FOR ORGANS, PIANOS & ELECTRONIC KEYBOARDS

DANCE BAND GREATS

4

E-Z does it! That's why E-Z Play TODAY Music was created. This series has been designed with a special music notation for instant playing enjoyment.

The collection of songs in each book has been specifically arranged for use with all major brand organs, including chord organs and those with automatic chord units. Special chord notation is also included for the triad and conventional chord player. The entire series provides a play-on-sight repertoire filled with musical fun for everyone . . . delightful tunes that will appeal to every musical interest.

Before you begin your "E-Z" adventure, read the next two pages for a "playing preview" of the special notation and a full explanation of the chord symbols used throughout the series. If this is your first encounter with organ music, you'll be able to enjoy instant playing fun. If you've had previous organ playing experience, you'll enjoy having a complete variety of music at your fingertips. In any case, there are hours of musical fun ahead for everyone.

Contents

HAL•LEONARD®
CORPORATION
7777 W. BLUEMOUND RD. P.O. BOX 13819 MILWAUKEE, WI 53213

T0050966

Playing Preview

THE MELODY (Right Hand)

The melody of a song appears as large lettered notes on a staff. The letter name corresponds to a key on the keyboard of an organ.

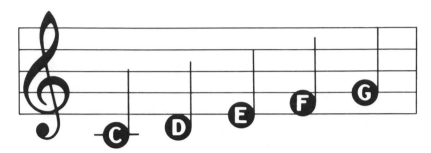

ACCOMPANIMENT (Left Hand)

The arrangements in this series have been written for all types of chord accompaniment.

1 One button (chord organ) or one-key chords.

2 Three-note (triad) chords.

3 Conventional, or standard chord positions.

Chord names, called chord symbols, appear above the melody line as either a boxed symbol [C]

or as an alternate chord (C7)

or both C7/[C]

1 For chord organ or one-key chords, play whichever chord name is on your unit.

2 If you are playing triad chords, follow the boxed symbols. A triad chord is played like this:

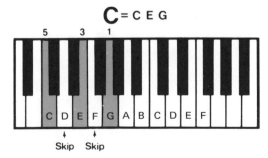

- Place your little finger on the key which has the same letter name as the chord.
- Skip a white key and place your middle finger on the next white key.
- Skip another white key and place your thumb on the next white key.

In some cases, there is an ARROW to the **left** or to the **right** of the chord name.

The arrow indicates moving one of the triad notes either to the **left** or to the **right** on the keyboard.

To understand this, first think of a chord symbol as having three sections, representing the three notes of the chord.

An ARROW is positioned next to the chord letter in one of these sections, indicating which of the three notes to change. For example:

• An arrow to the left means to move a note of the chord **down** (left) to the next adjacent key.

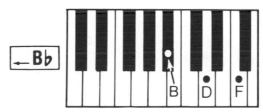

In this example where the arrow is in the **lower left**, or "1" position, move the first note "B" **down** to the black key B♭.

• An arrow to the right means to move a note of the chord **up** (right) to the next adjacent key.

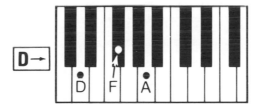

In this example where the arrow is in the **middle**, or "2" position, move the middle note **up** to the black key F♯.

3 If you are playing standard chord positions, play the chord in the boxed symbol, unless an alternate chord is indicated. Play alternate chords whenever possible.

For your reference, a Chord Speller Chart of standard chord positions appears in the back of this book.

REGISTRATION AND RHYTHM

A Registration number is shown above the music for each song. This number corresponds to the same number on the Registration Guide which appears on the inside front cover of this book. The Registration numbers also correspond to the numbers on the E-Z Play TODAY Registration Guides that are available for many brands of organs. See your organ dealer for the details.

You may wish to select your own favorite registration or perhaps experiment with different voice combinations. Then add an automatic rhythm...and HAVE FUN.

Cherry Pink And Apple Blossom White

Words by Jacques La Rue
English Words by Mack David
Music by Louiguy

Registration 9

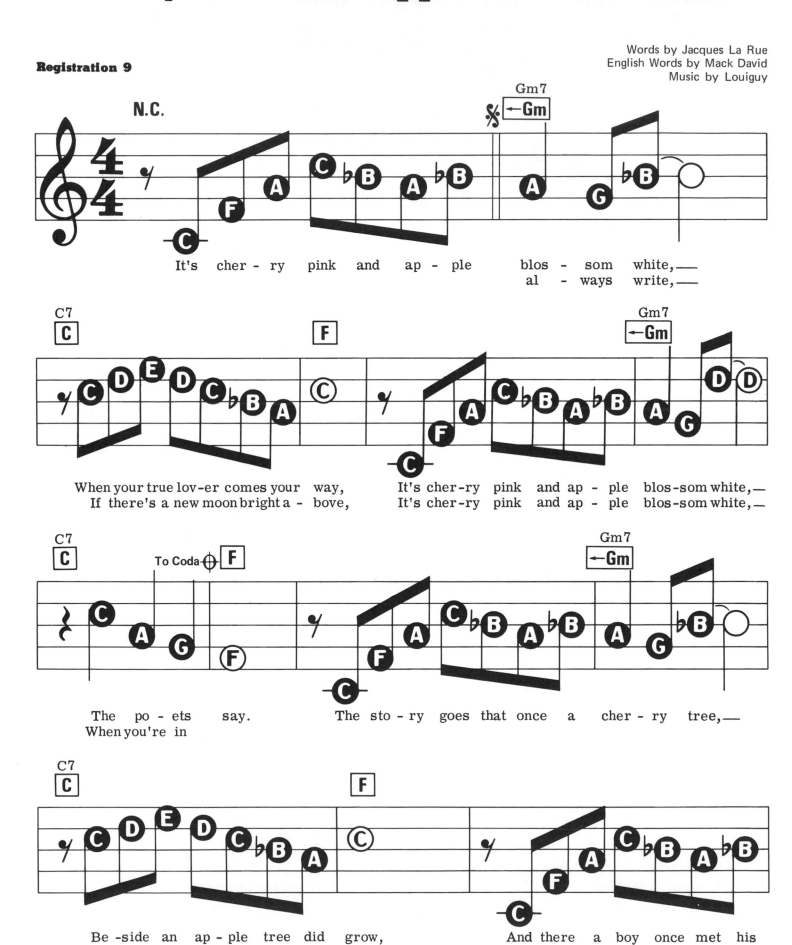

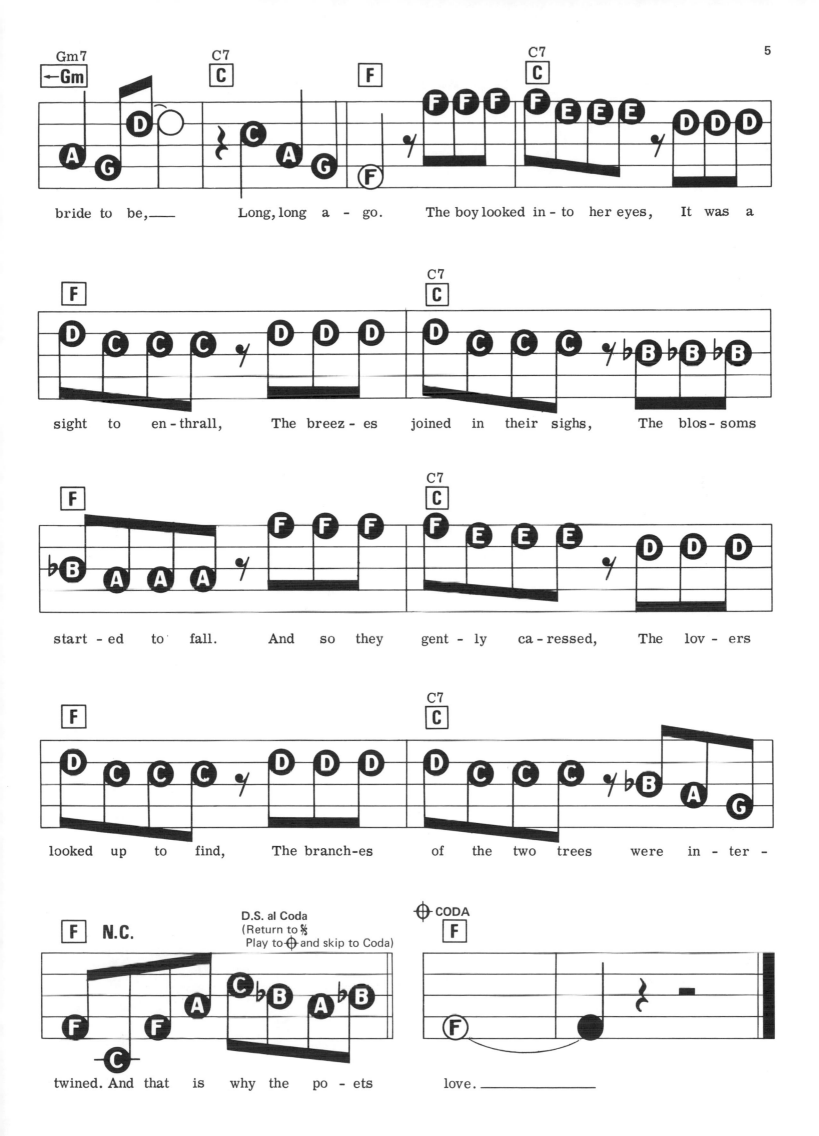

Cotton Fields
(The Cotton Song)

Words and Music by
Huddie Ledbetter

Registration 8

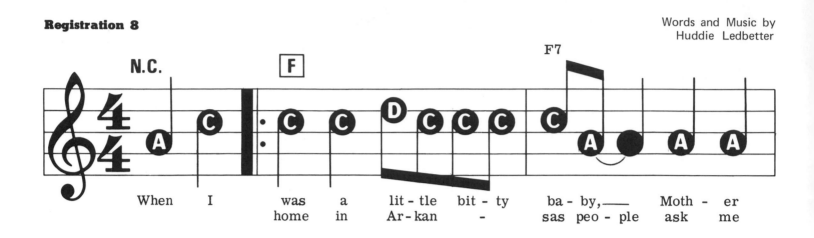

When I was a lit-tle bit-ty ba-by,____ Moth-er
home in Ar-kan - sas peo-ple ask me

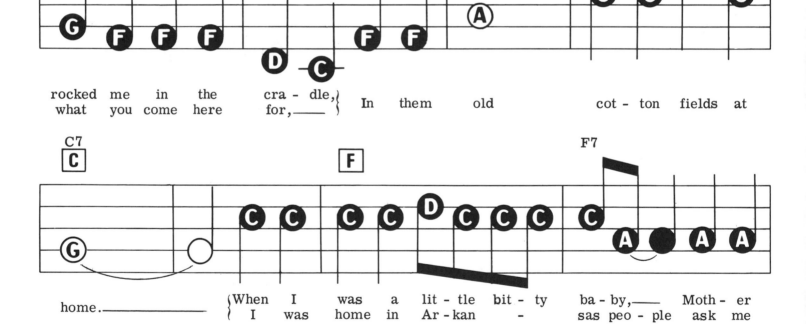

rocked me in the cra-dle,) In them old cot-ton fields at
what you come here for,____}

home._____ {When I was a lit-tle bit-ty ba-by,____ Moth-er
{ I was home in Ar-kan - sas peo-ple ask me

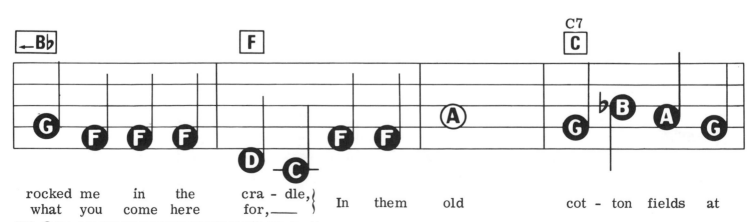

rocked me in the cra-dle,) In them old cot-ton fields at
what you come here for,____}

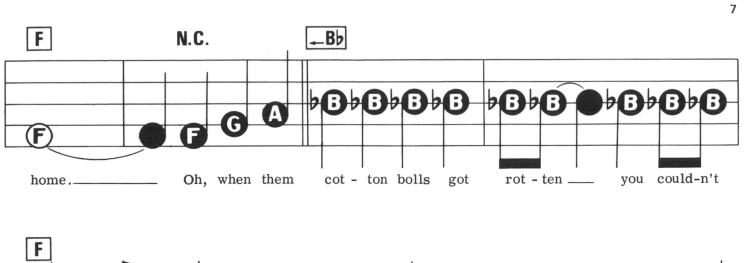

home. _____ Oh, when them cot - ton bolls got rot - ten _____ you could-n't

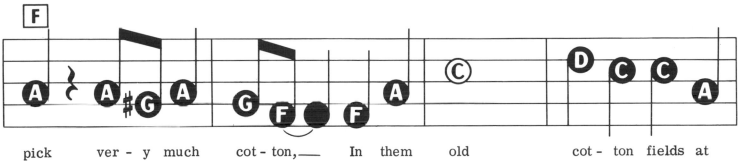

pick ver - y much cot - ton, ___ In them old cot - ton fields at

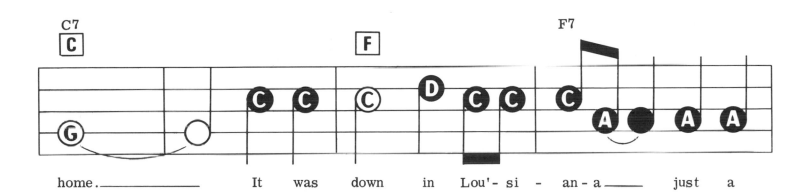

home. _____ It was down in Lou'- si - an-a _____ just a

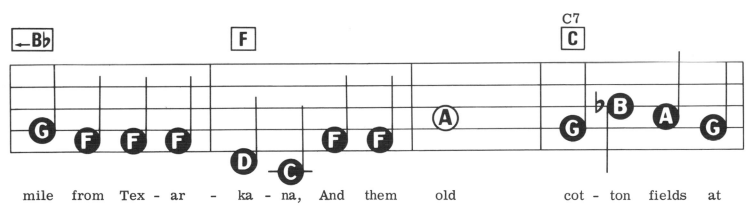

mile from Tex - ar - ka - na, And them old cot - ton fields at

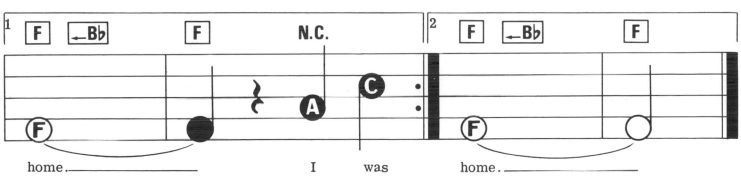

home. _____ I was home. _____

Exactly Like You

Registration 7

Words by Dorothy Fields
Music by Jimmy McHugh

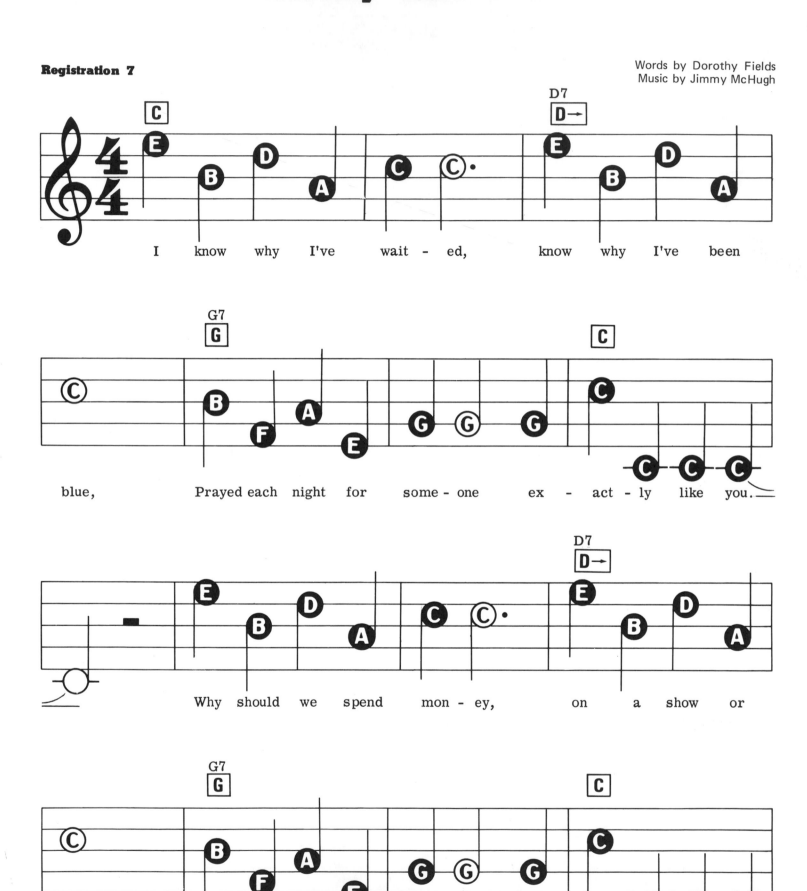

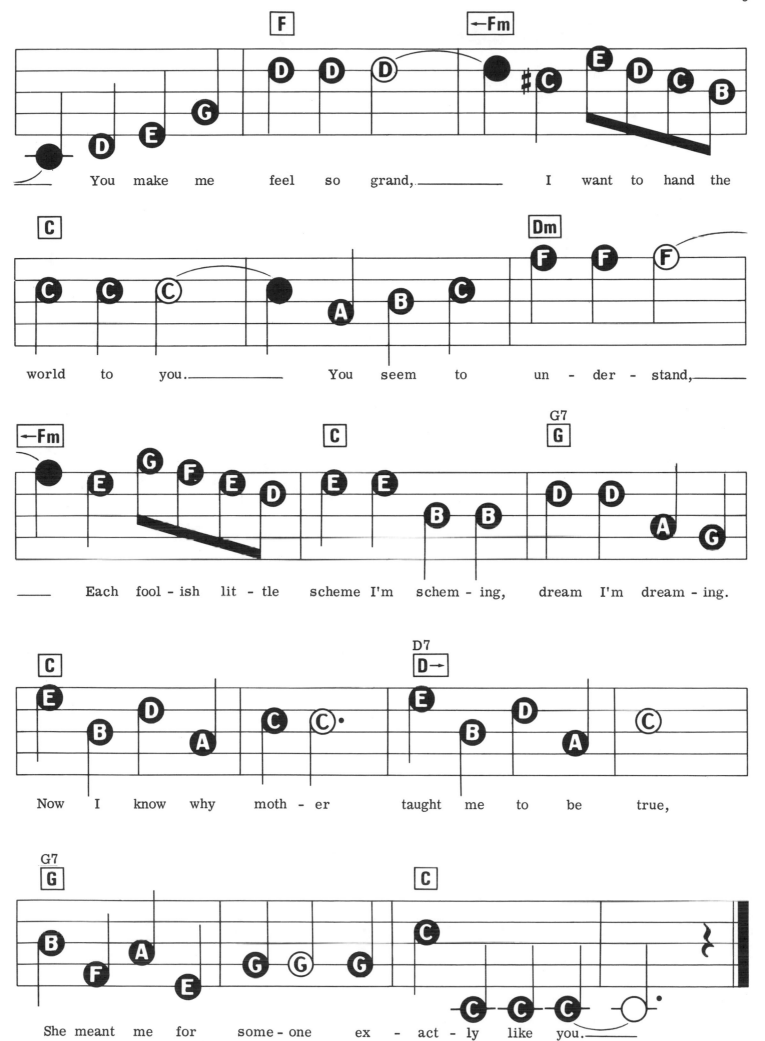

Fly Me To The Moon
(In Other Words)

Registration 2

Words and Music by
Bart Howard

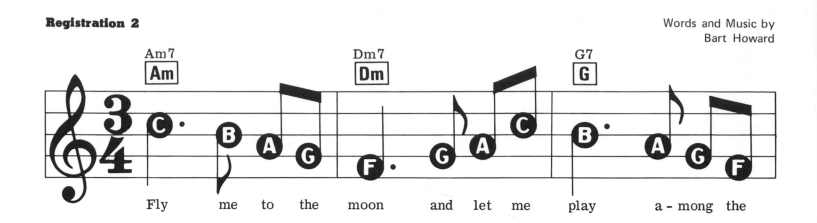

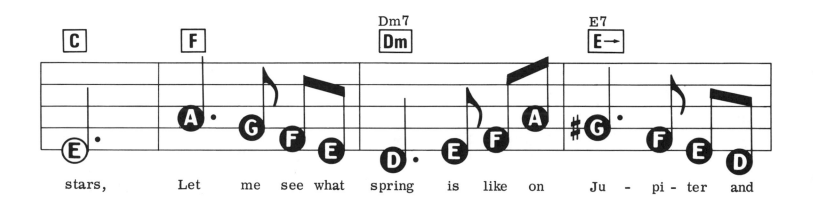

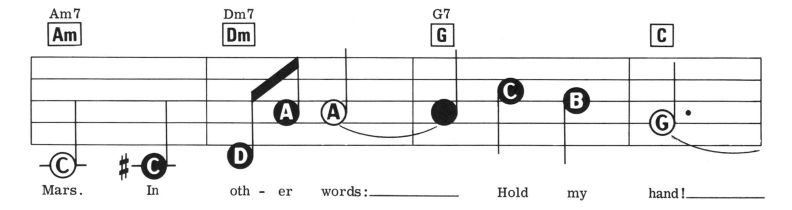

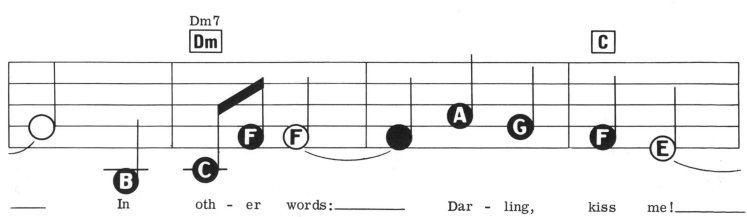

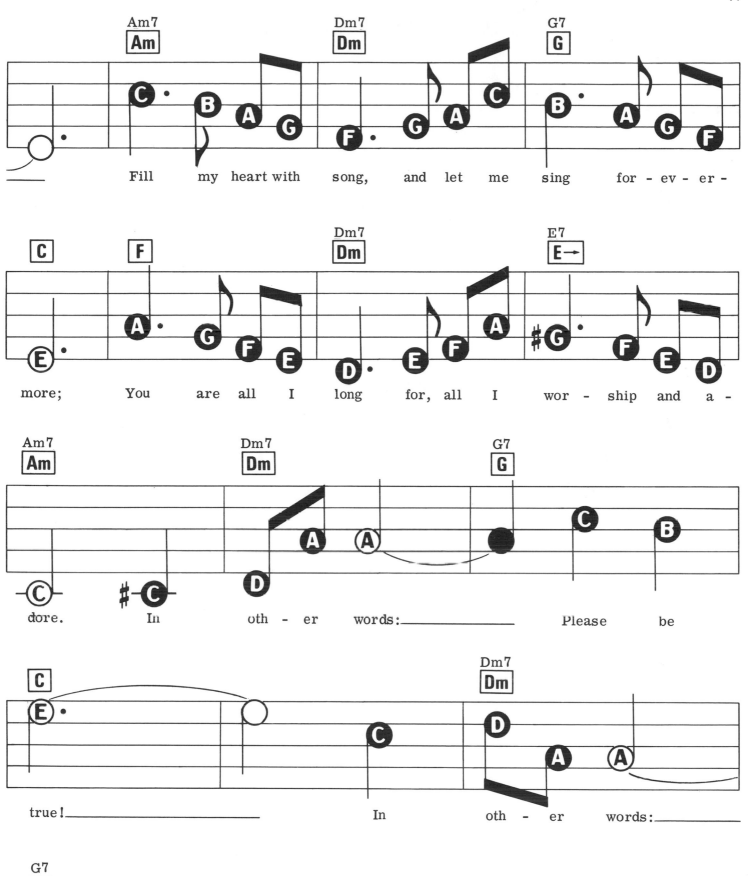

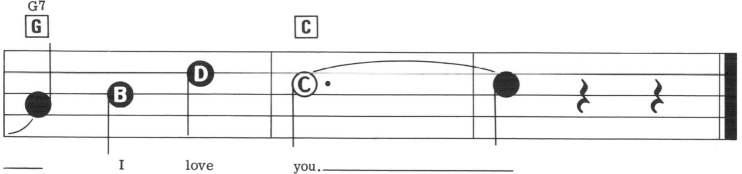

The Glory Of Love

Registration 3

Words and Music by
Billy Hill

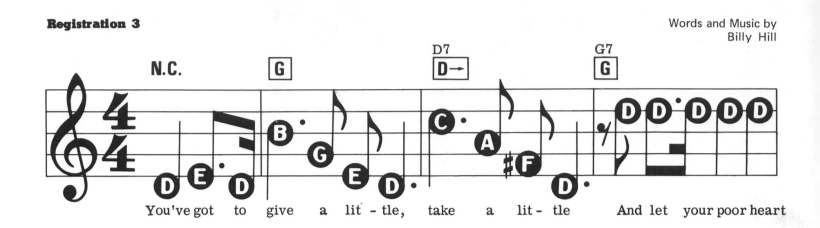

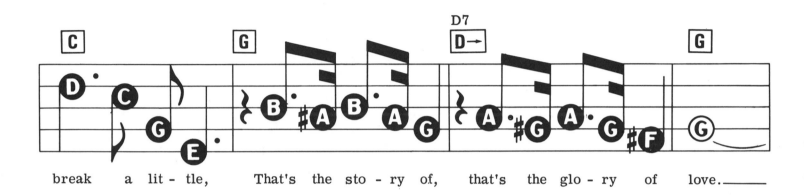

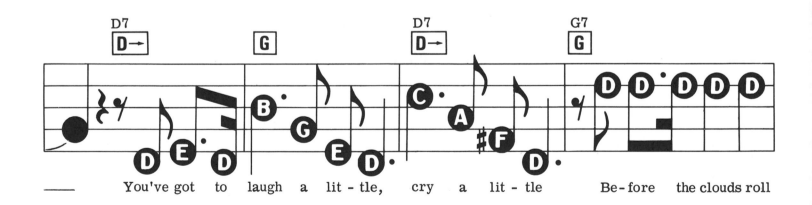

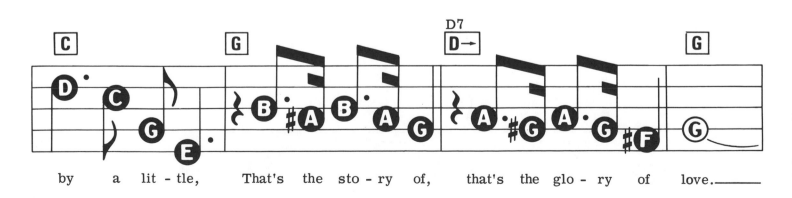

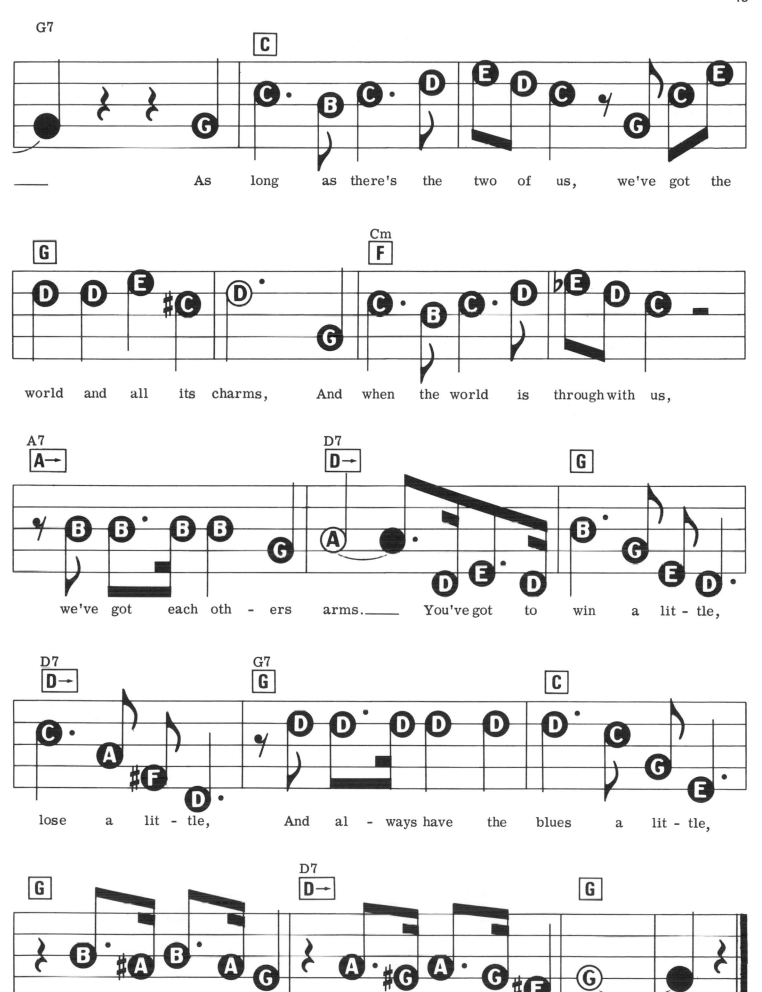

Goodnight, Irene

Registration 10

Words and Music by Huddie Ledbetter &
John A. Lomax

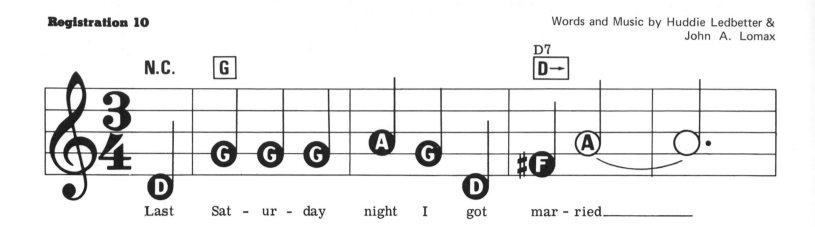

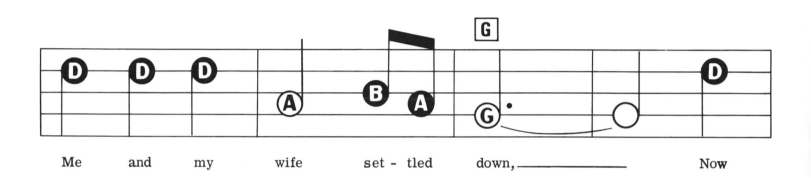

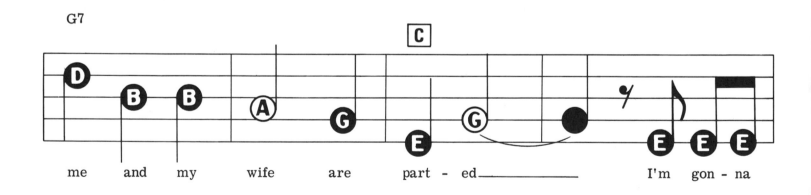

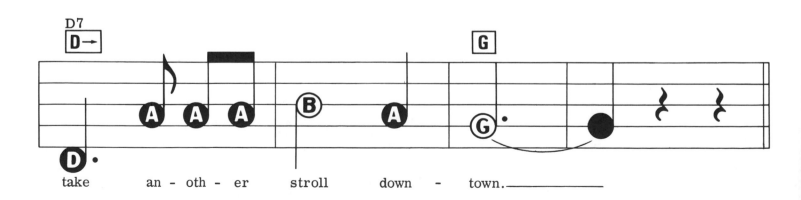

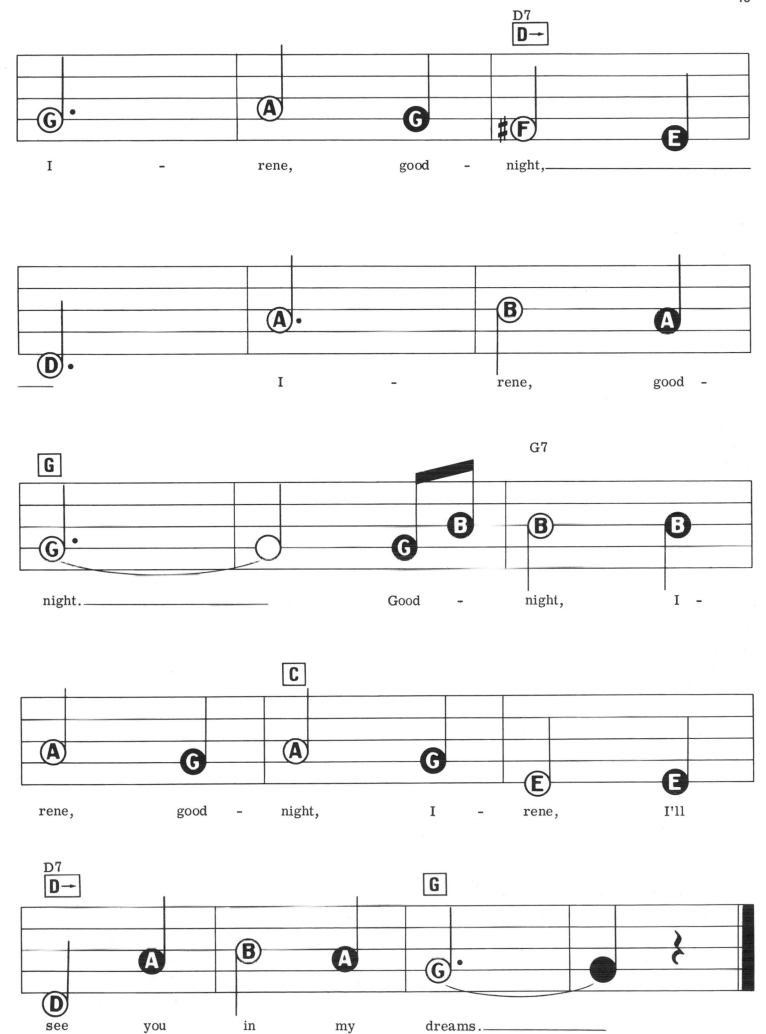

Harbor Lights

Registration 2

Words and Music by Jimmy Kennedy &
Hugh Williams

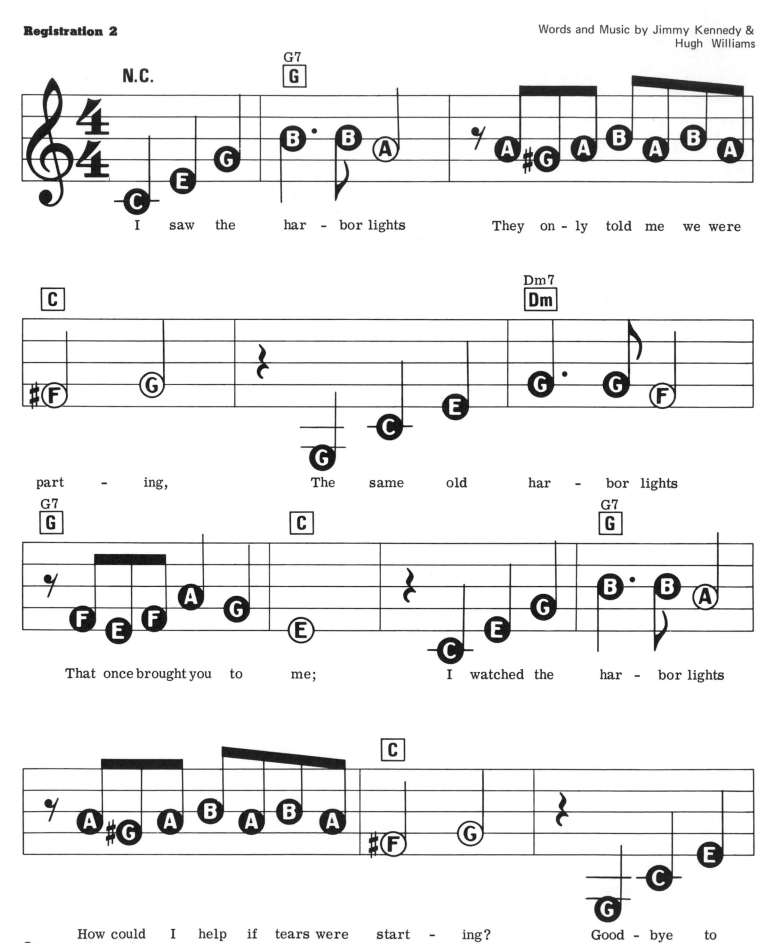

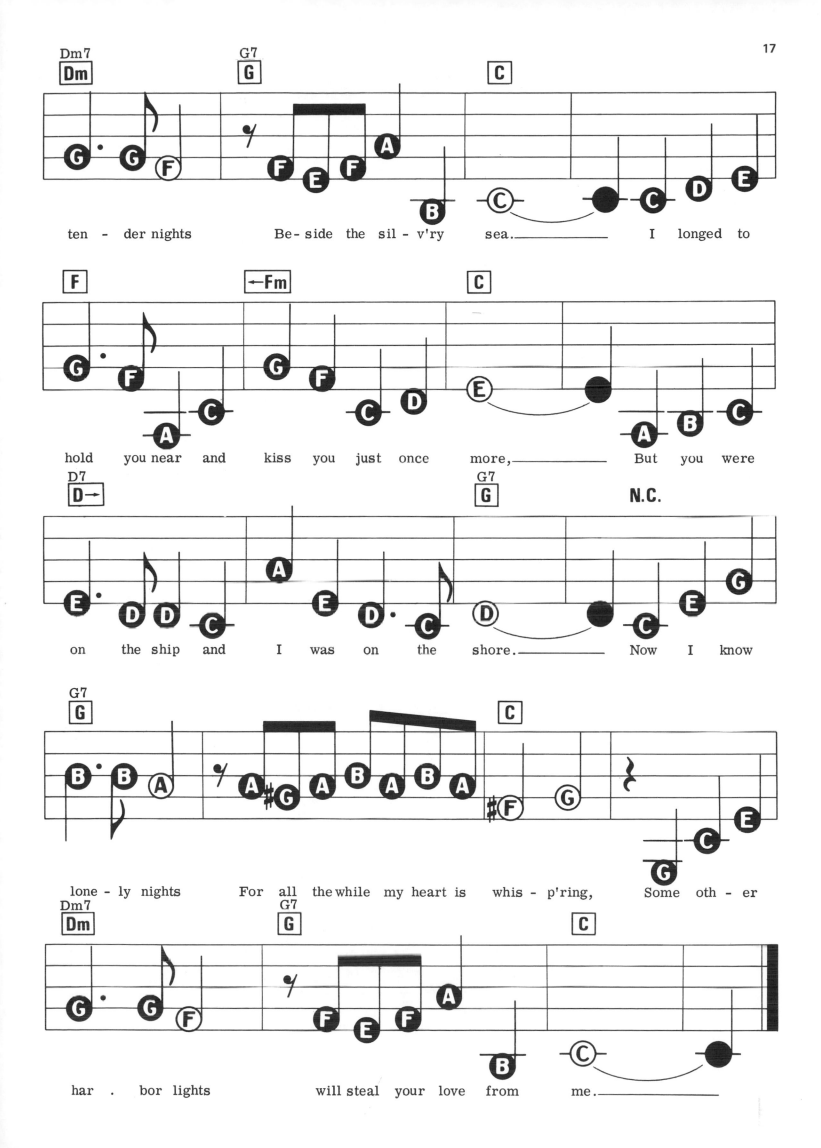

In The Mood

(Song)

Registration 8

Words and Music by
Joe Garland

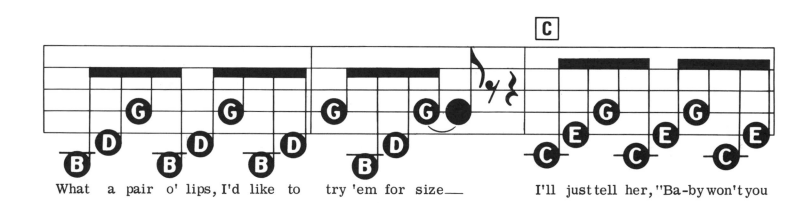

Who's the liv-in' dol-ly with the beau-ti-ful eyes—

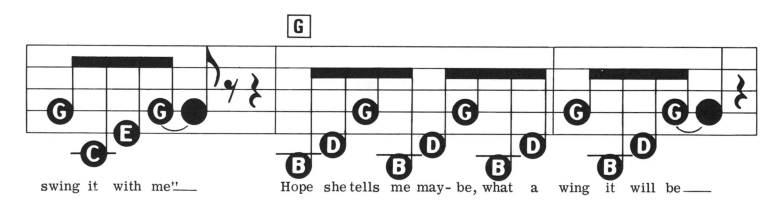

What a pair o' lips, I'd like to try 'em for size— I'll just tell her, "Ba-by won't you

swing it with me"— Hope she tells me may-be, what a wing it will be—

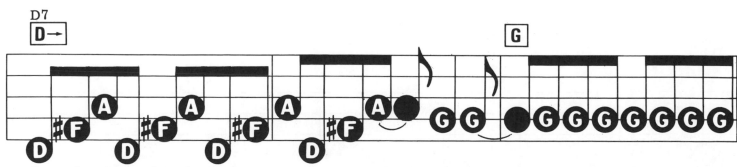

So, I said po-lite-ly, "Dar-lin' may I in-trude"— She said—"Don't keep me wait-in' when I'm

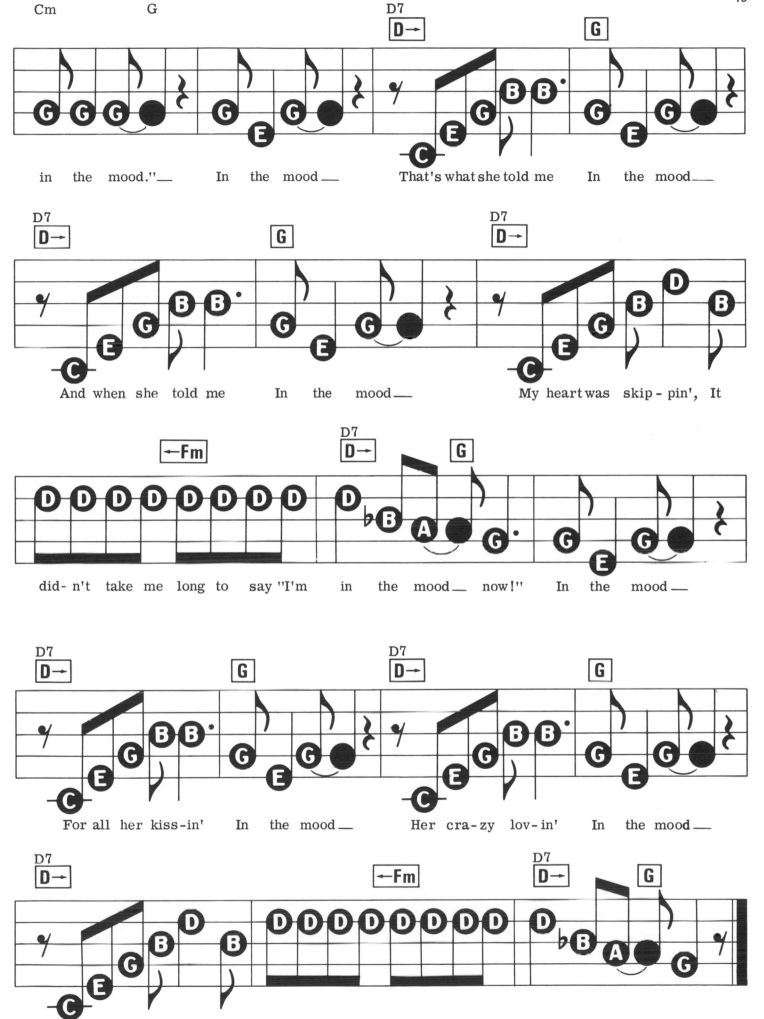

Love Me Or Leave Me

Words by Gus Kahn
Music by Walter Donaldson

Registration 7

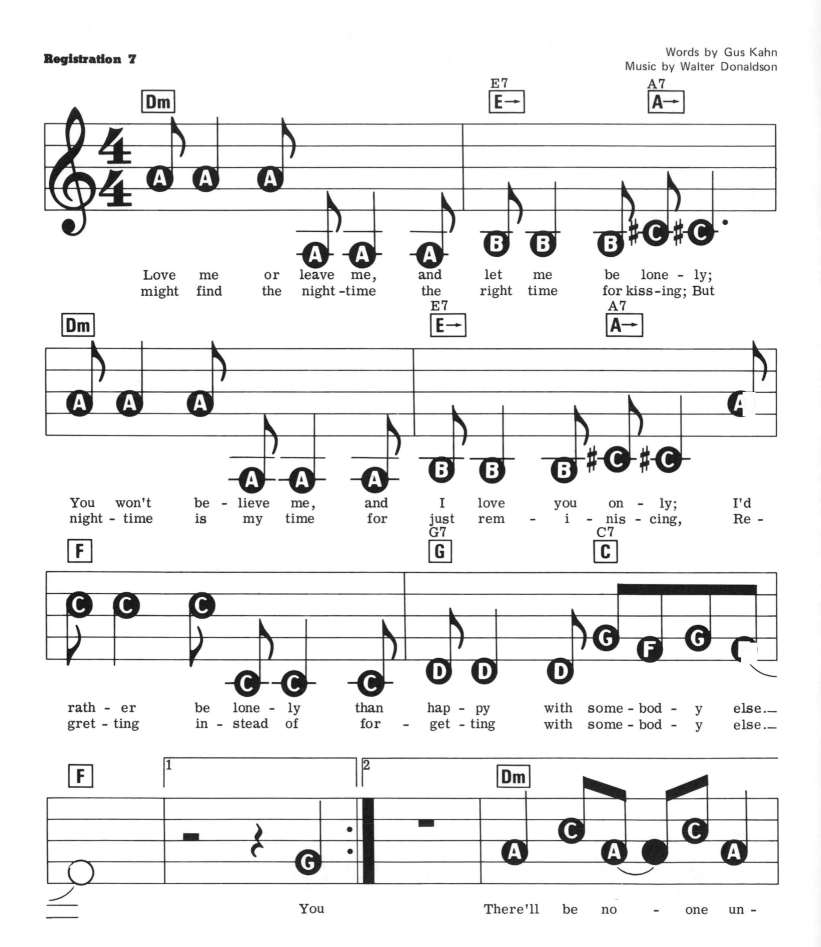

21

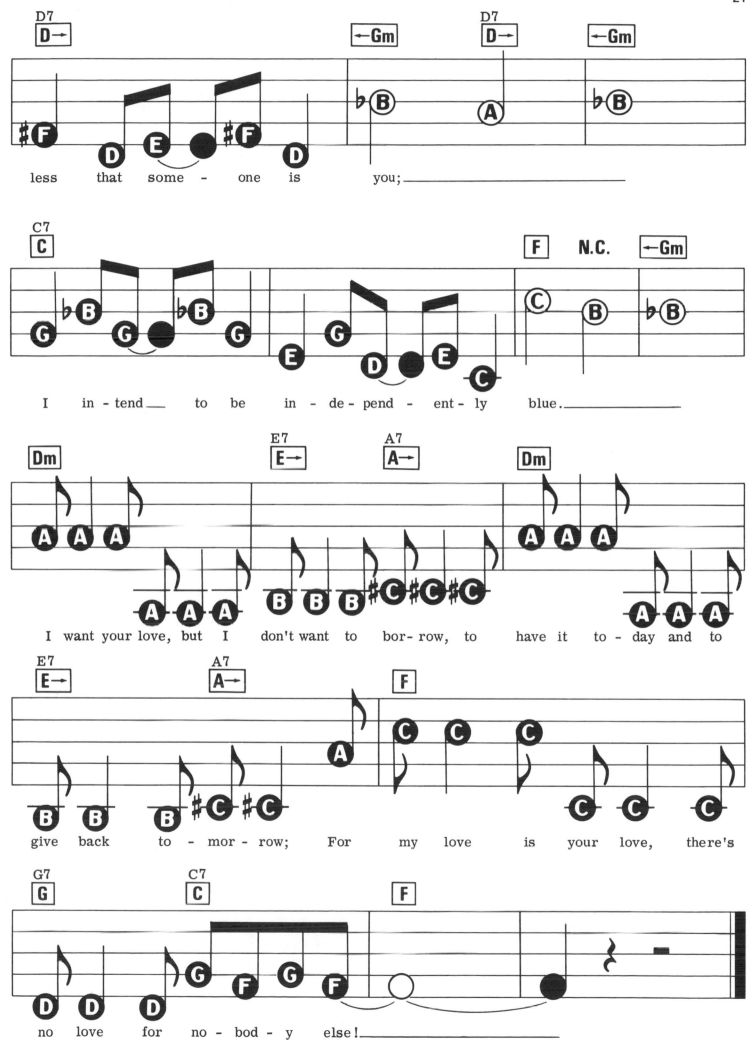

On The Sunny Side Of The Street

Registration 7

Words by Dorothy Fields
Music by Jimmy McHugh

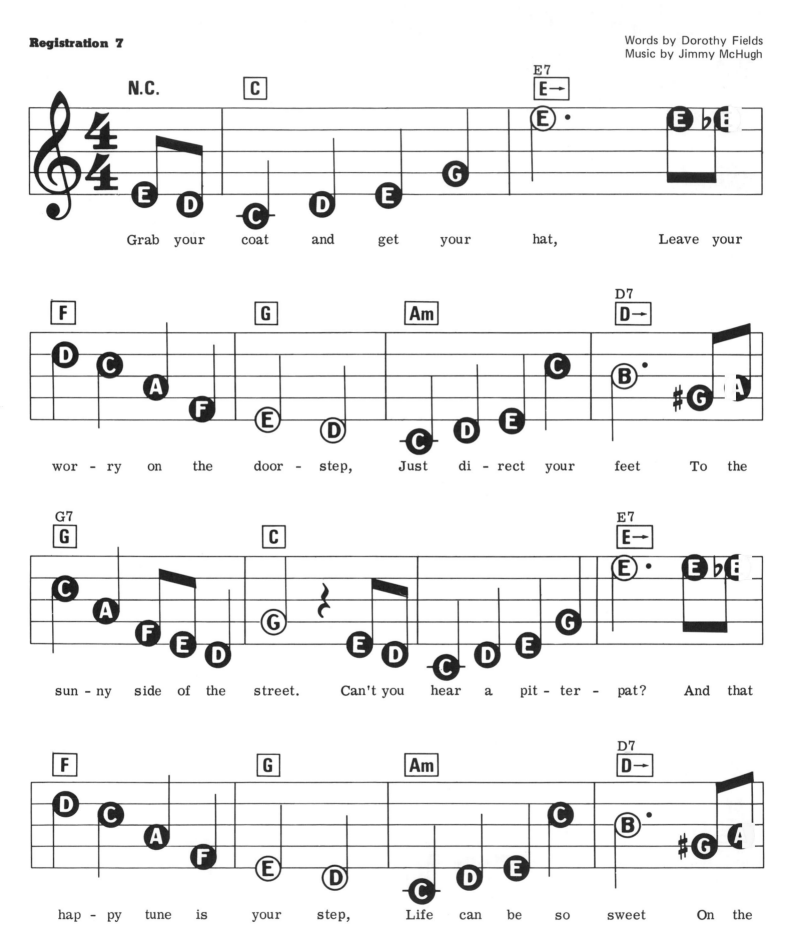

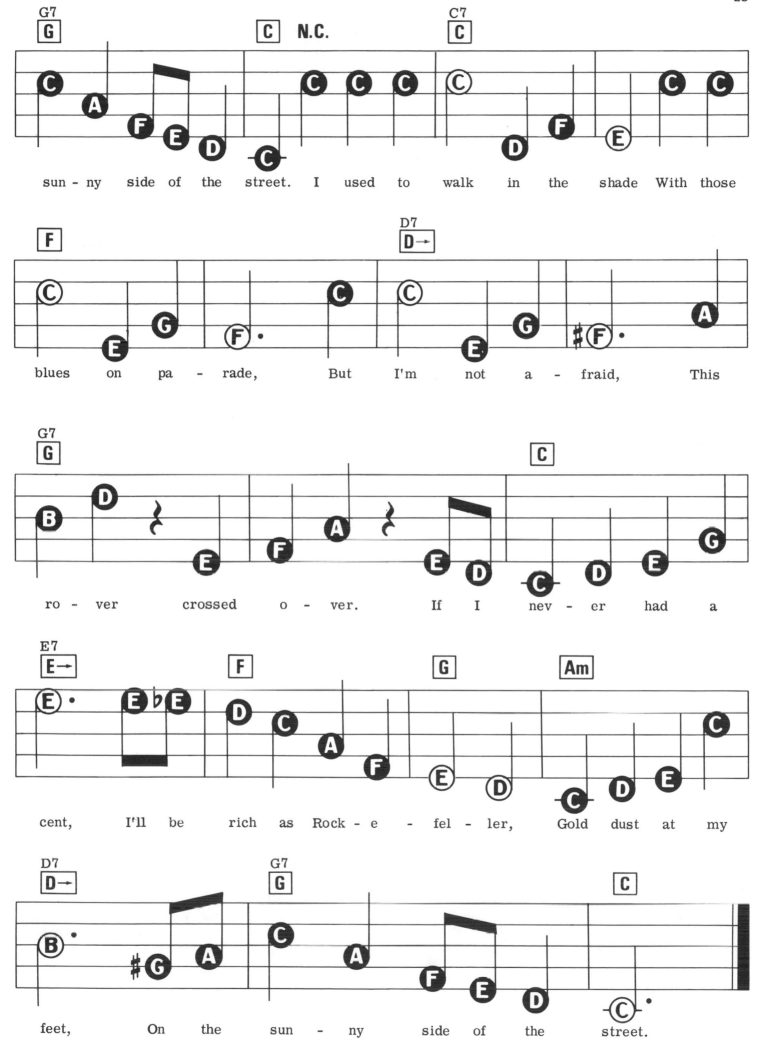

Paper Doll

Registration 4

Words and Music by
Johnny S. Black

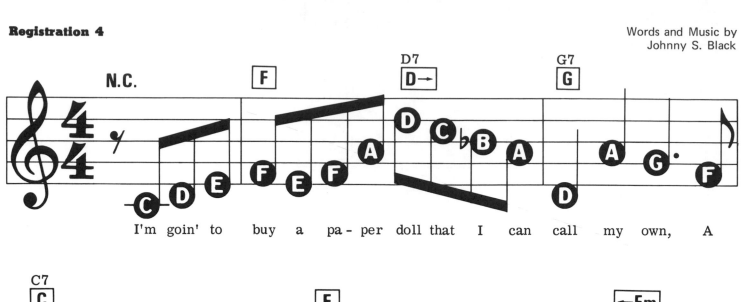

I'm goin' to buy a pa-per doll that I can call my own, A

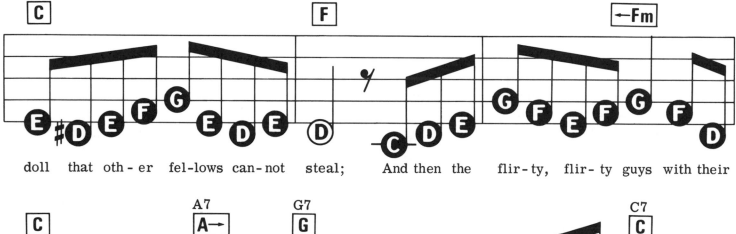

doll that oth-er fel-lows can-not steal; And then the flir-ty, flir-ty guys with their

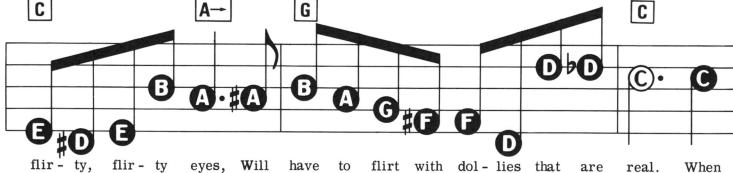

flir-ty, flir-ty eyes, Will have to flirt with dol-lies that are real. When

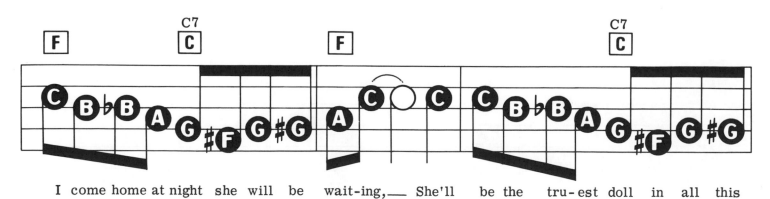

I come home at night she will be wait-ing,— She'll be the tru-est doll in all this

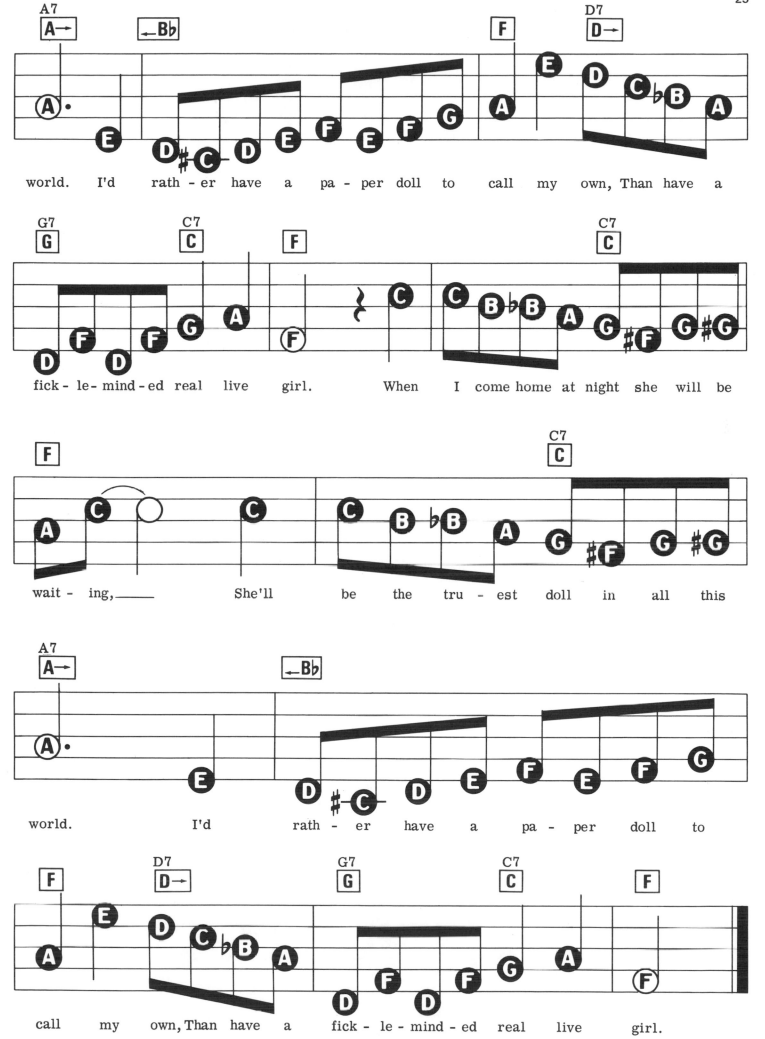

September Song

Words by Maxwell Anderson
Music by Kurt Weill

Registration 2

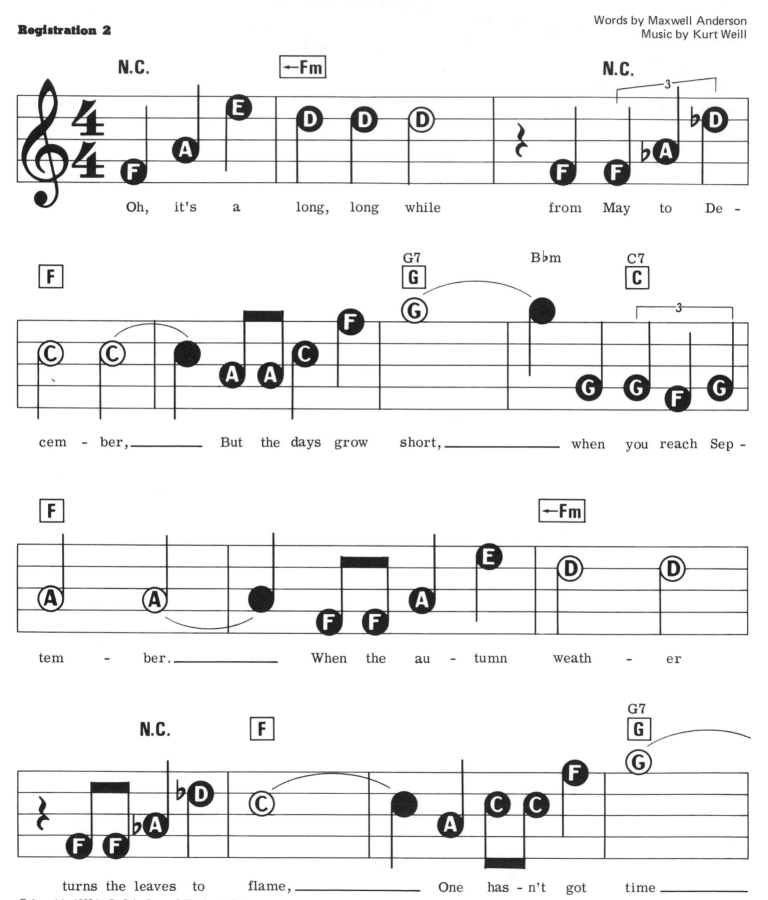

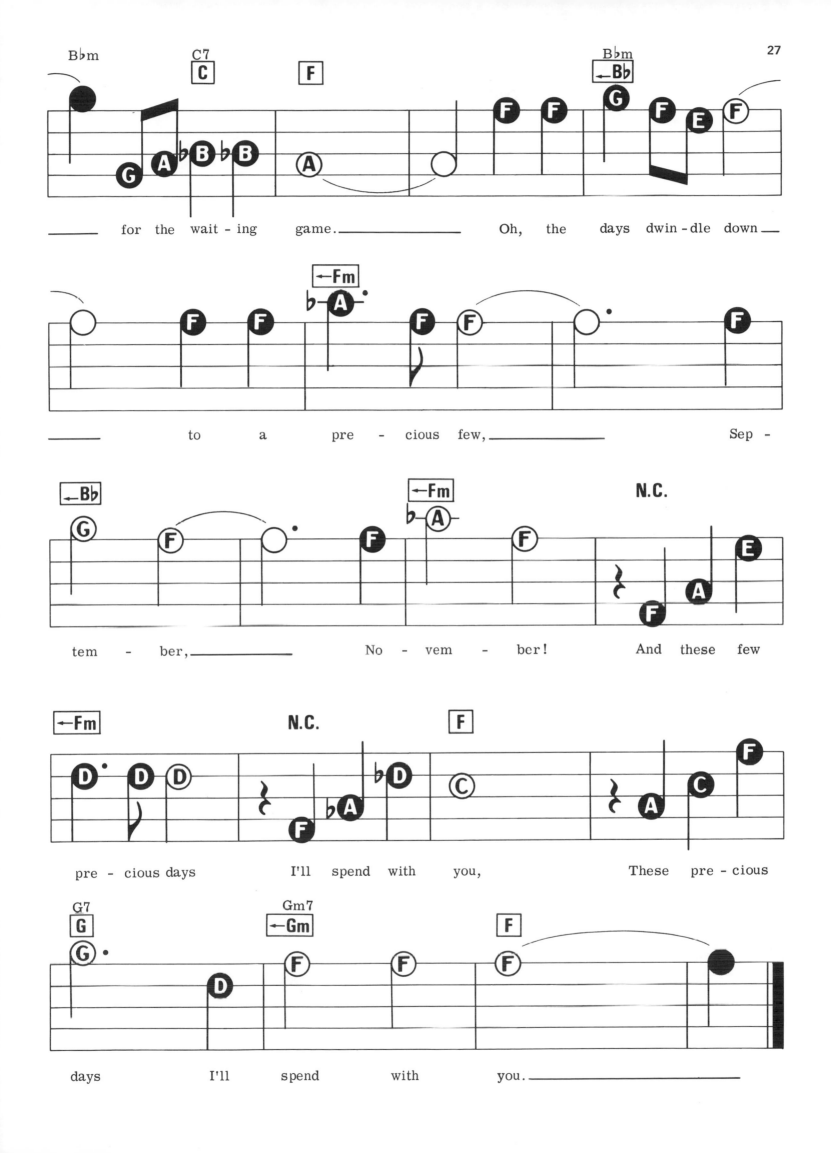

Side By Side

Registration 7

Words and Music by
Harry Woods

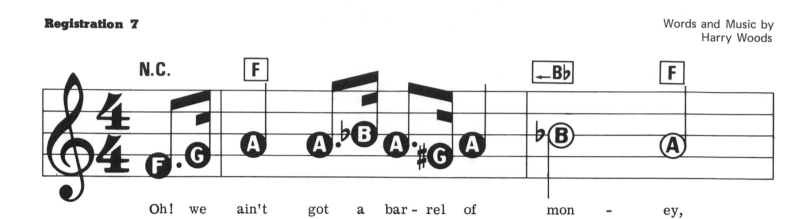

Oh! we ain't got a bar-rel of mon - ey,

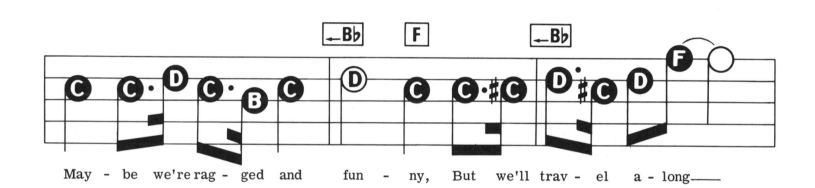

May - be we're rag - ged and fun - ny, But we'll trav - el a - long

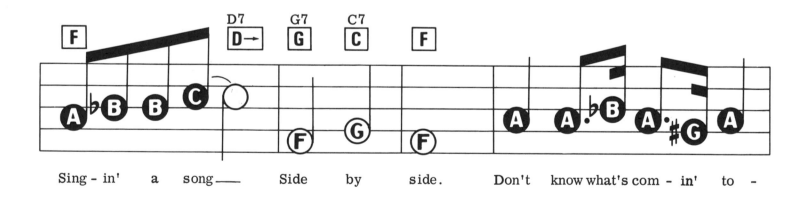

Sing - in' a song Side by side. Don't know what's com - in' to -

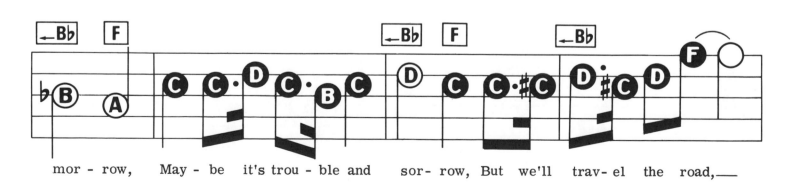

mor - row, May - be it's trou - ble and sor - row, But we'll trav - el the road,

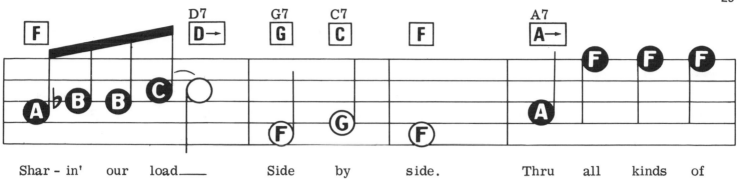

Shar - in' our load___ Side by side. Thru all kinds of

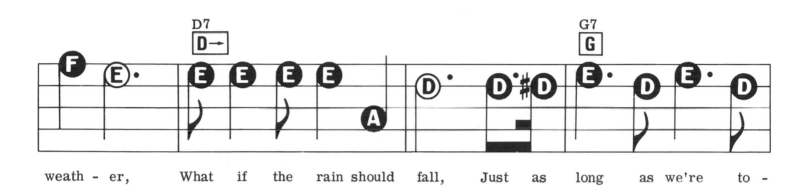

weath - er, What if the rain should fall, Just as long as we're to -

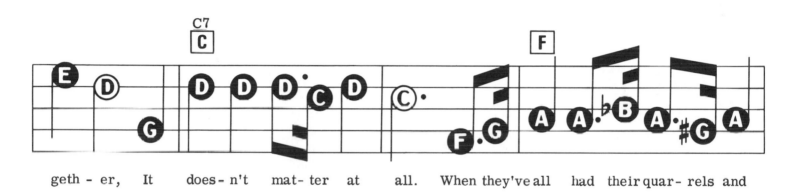

geth - er, It does - n't mat - ter at all. When they've all had their quar - rels and

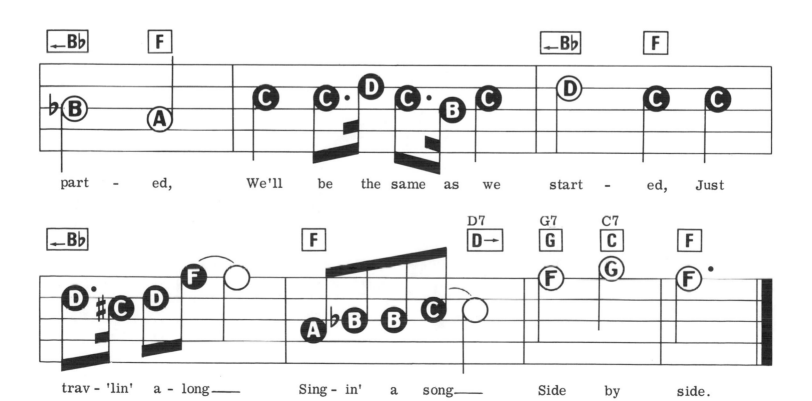

part - ed, We'll be the same as we start - ed, Just

trav - 'lin' a - long___ Sing - in' a song___ Side by side.

Soft Shoe Song
(Give Me That Old Soft Shoe)

Registration 8

By Roy Jordan
and Sid Bass

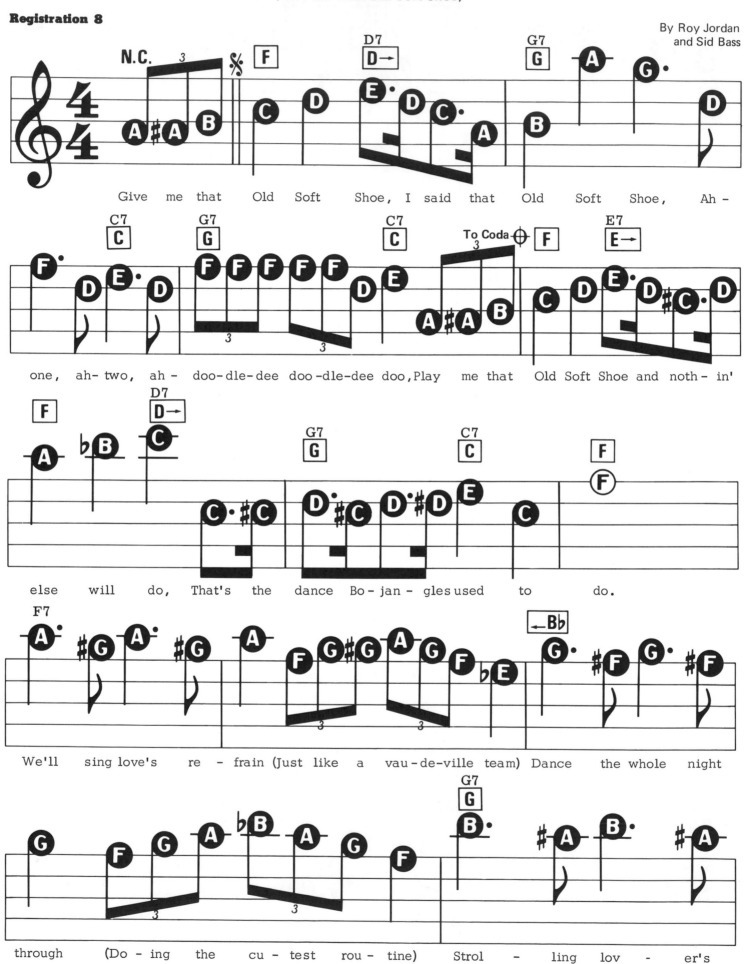

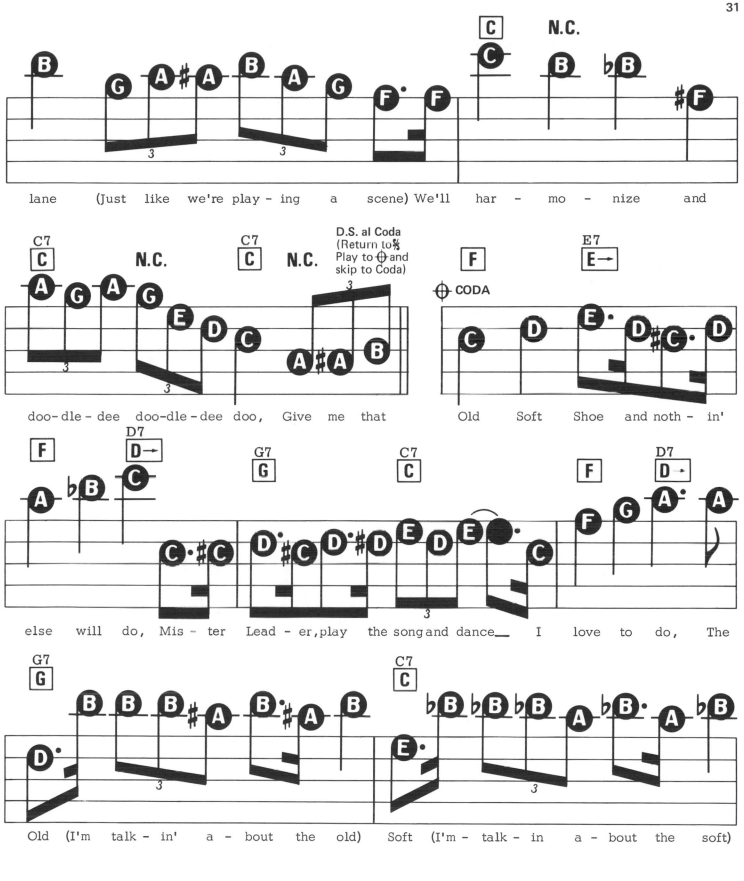

lane (Just like we're play-ing a scene) We'll har-mo-nize and

doo-dle-dee doo-dle-dee doo, Give me that Old Soft Shoe and noth-in'

else will do, Mis-ter Lead-er, play the song and dance___ I love to do, The

Old (I'm talk-in' a-bout the old) Soft (I'm-talk-in a-bout the soft)

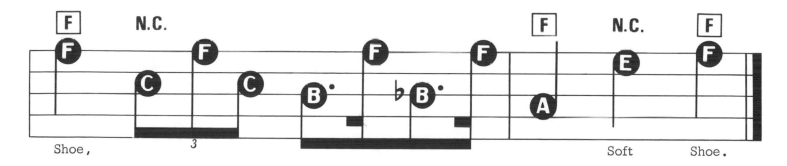

Shoe,   Soft Shoe.

Somebody Else Is Taking My Place

Registration 8

Words and Music by Dick Howard,
Bob Ellsworth & Russ Morgan

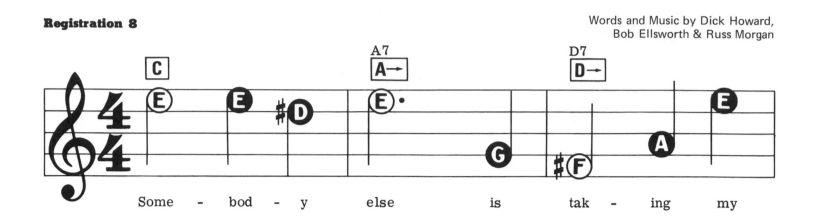

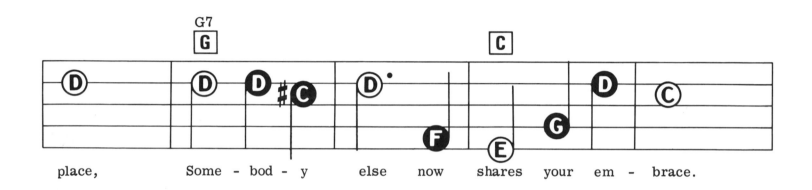

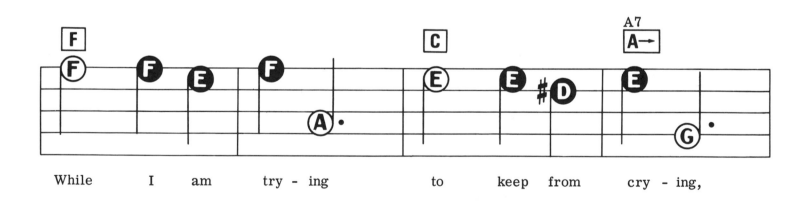

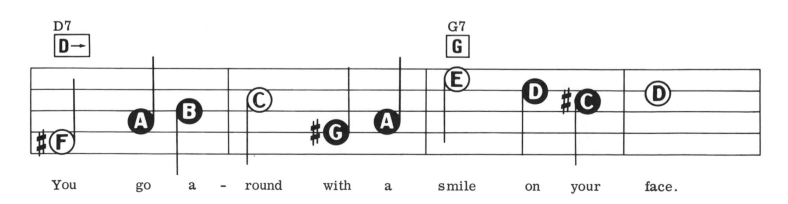

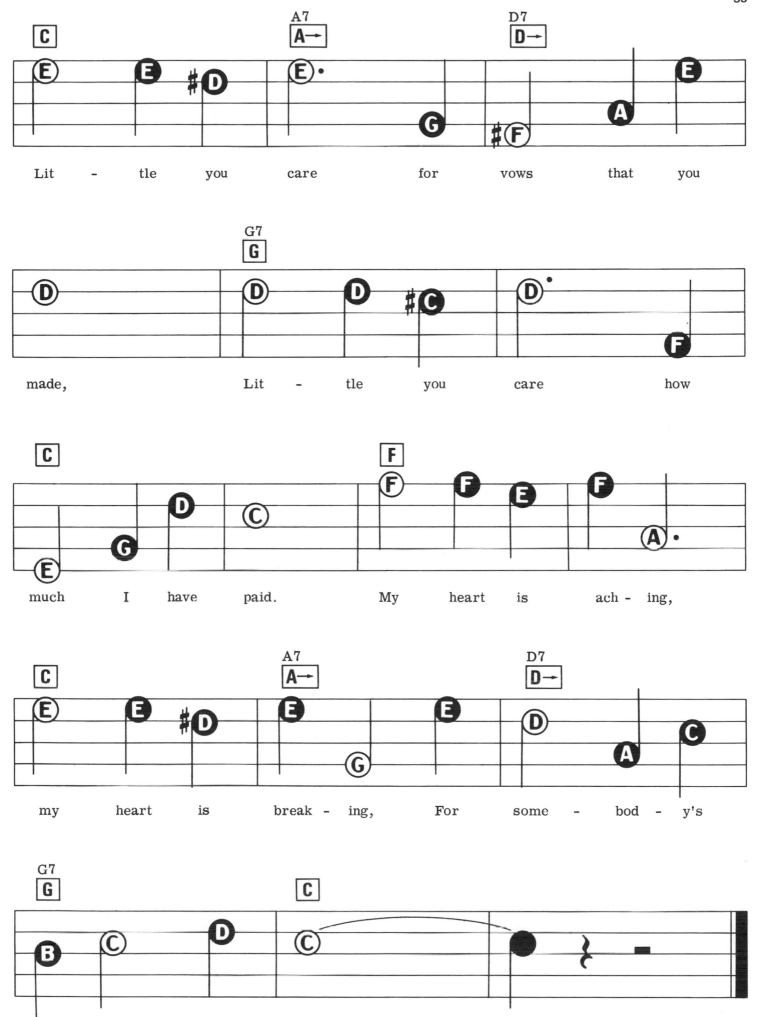

Sweet Sue – Just You

Words by Will J. Harris
Music by Victor Young

Registration 2

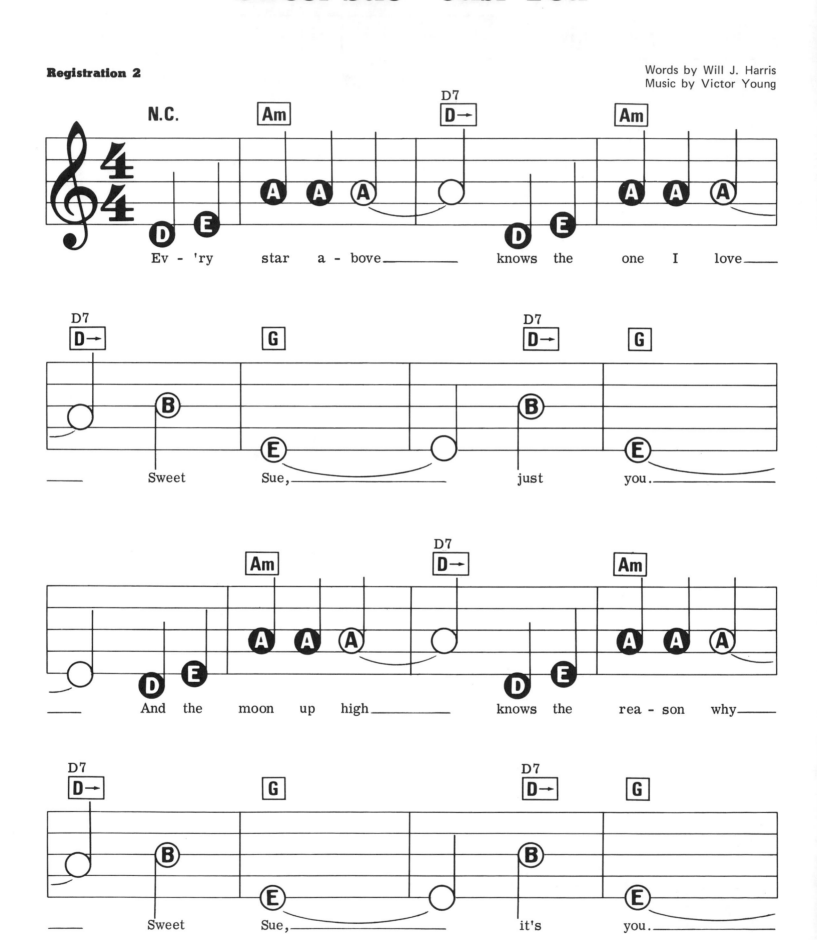

35

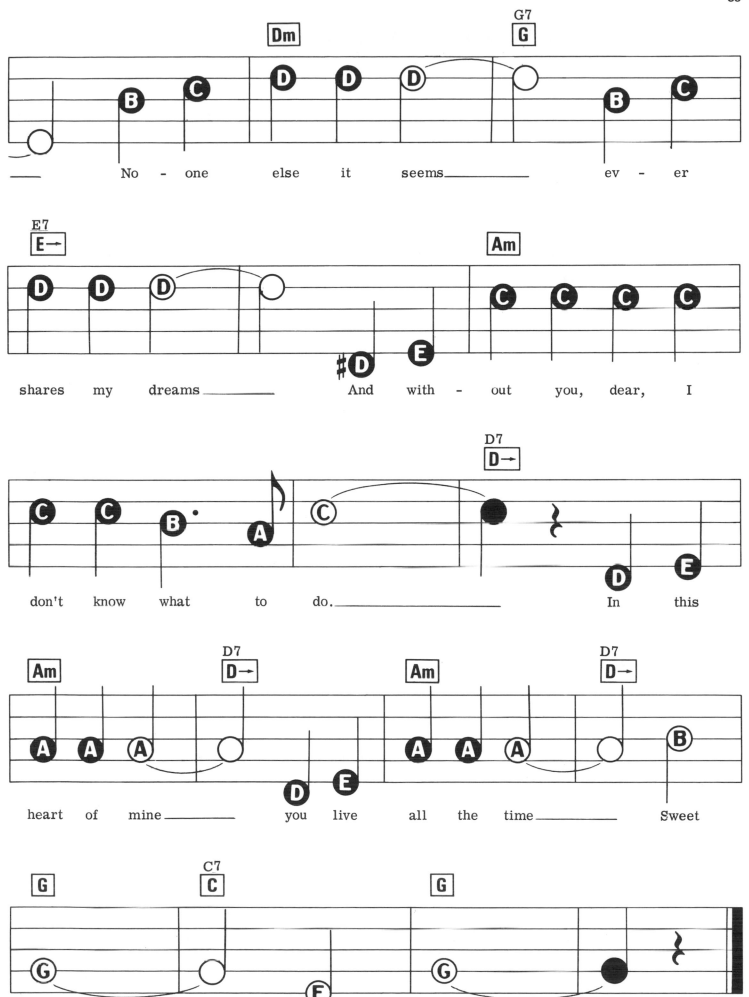

There'll Be Some Changes Made

Registration 7

Words by Billy Higgins
Music by W. Benton Overstreet

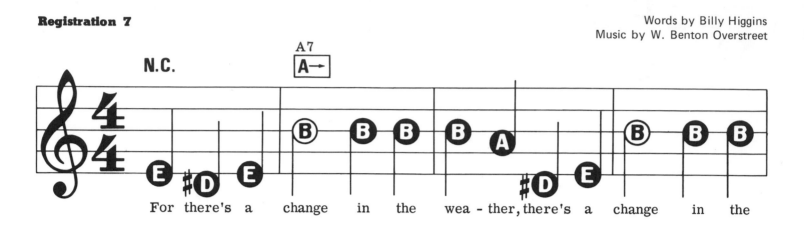

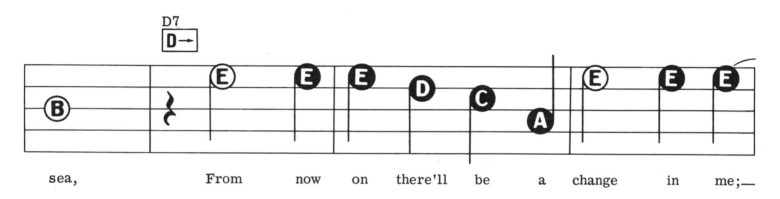

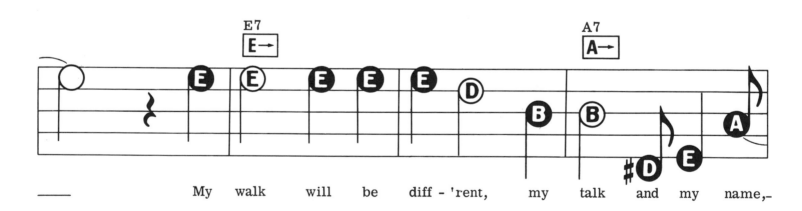

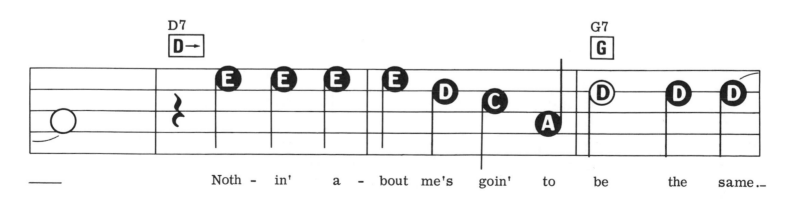

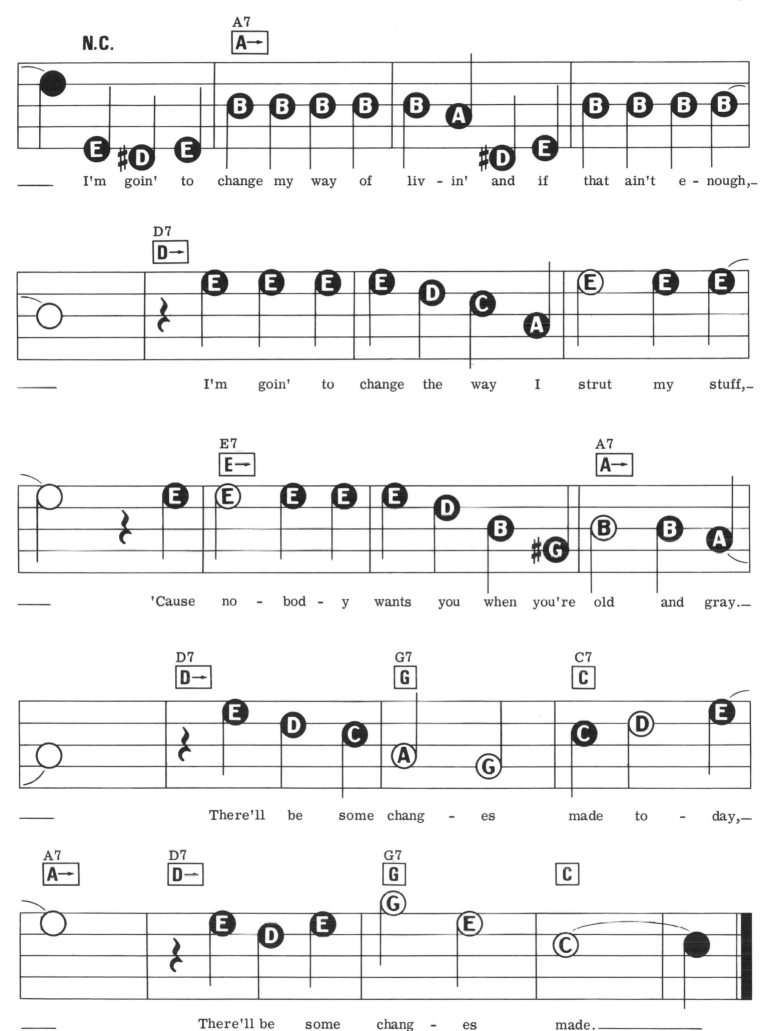

There's A Small Hotel

Registration 9

Words by Lorenz Hart
Music by Richard Rodgers

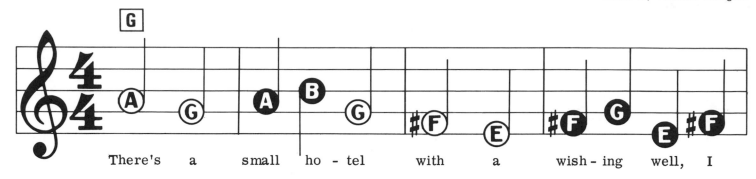

There's a small ho - tel with a wish - ing well, I

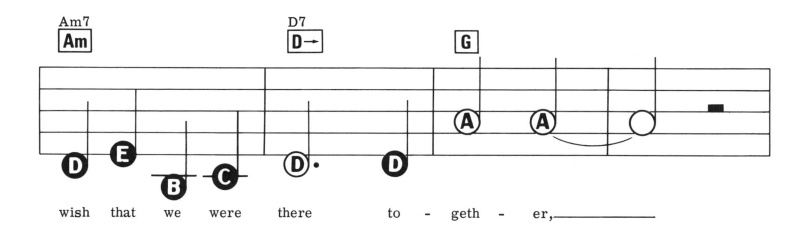

wish that we were there to - geth - er, _____

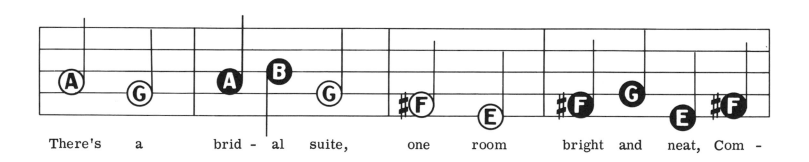

There's a brid - al suite, one room bright and neat, Com -

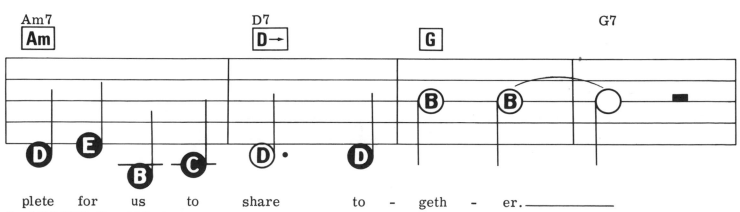

plete for us to share to - geth - er. _____

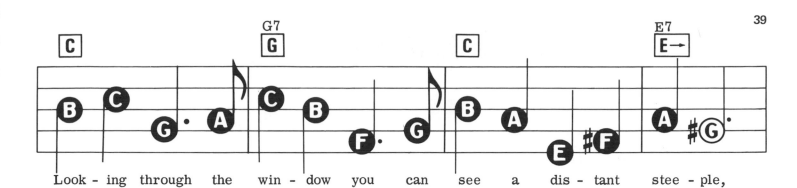

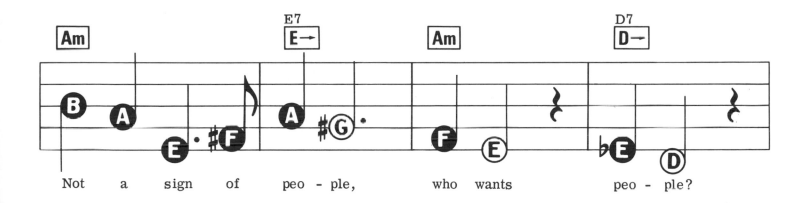

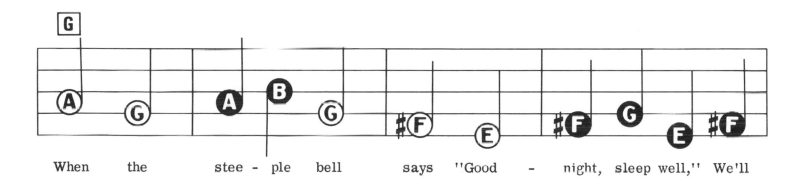

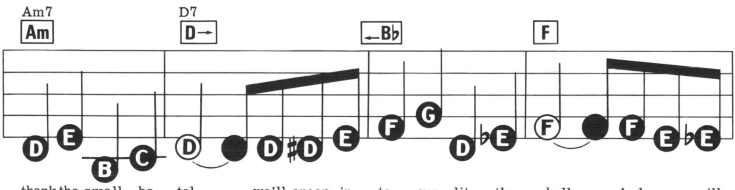

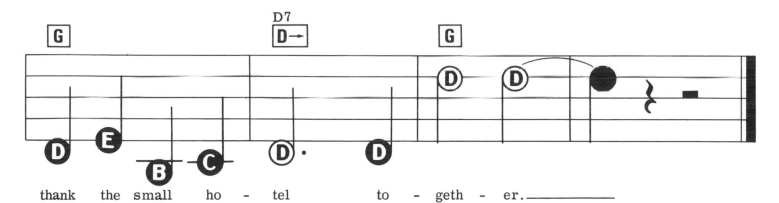

Things We Did Last Summer

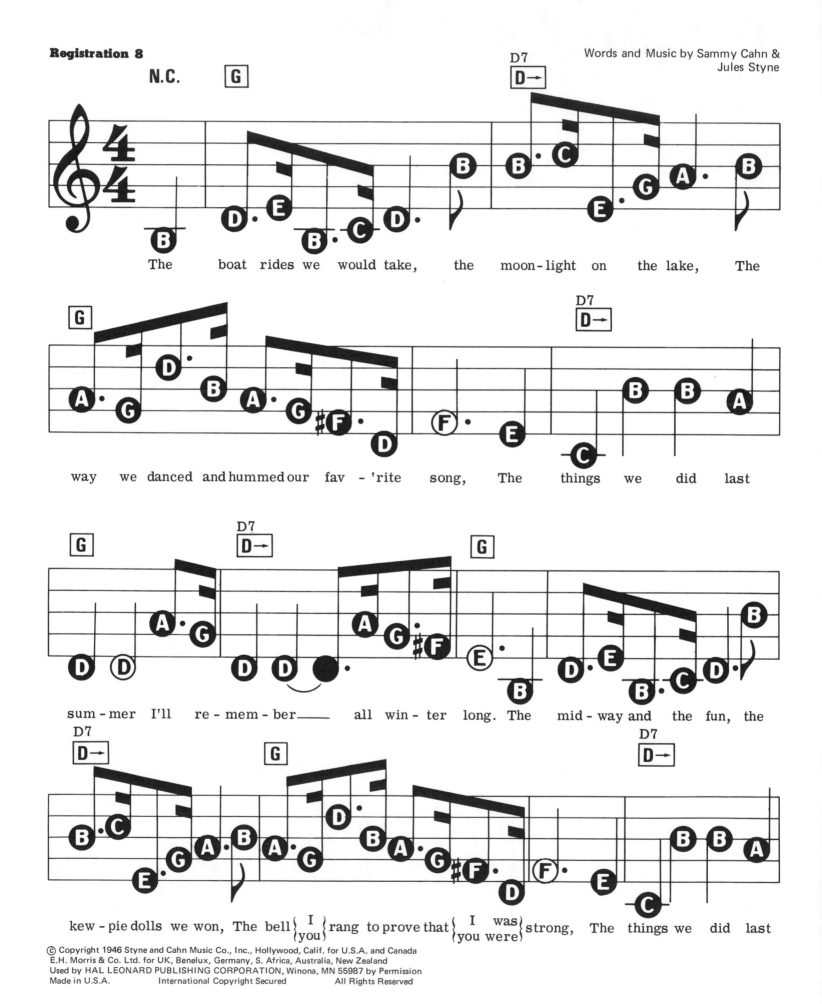

Registration 8

Words and Music by Sammy Cahn &
Jules Styne

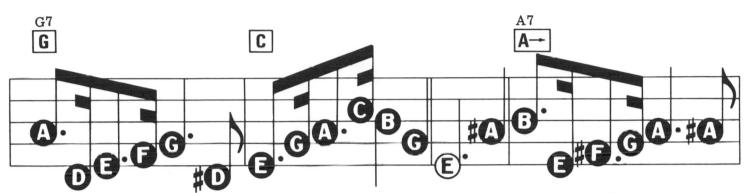

sum - mer I'll re - mem - ber___ all win - ter long. The ear - ly morn - ing hike, the

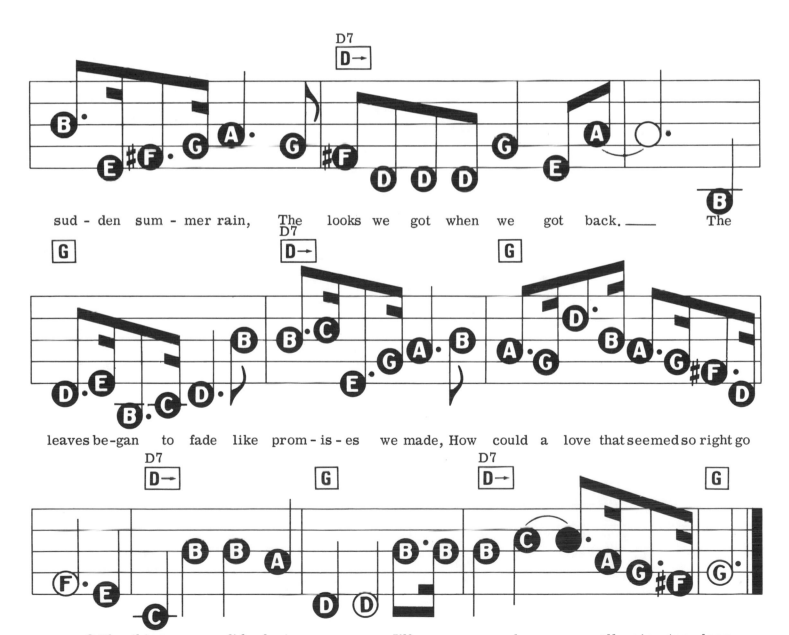

rent - ed tan - dem bike, The lunch - es that we used to pack; We nev - er could ex - plain that

sud - den sum - mer rain, The looks we got when we got back.___ The

leaves be - gan to fade like prom - is - es we made, How could a love that seemed so right go

wrong? The things we did last sum - mer I'll re - mem - ber___ all win - ter long.

Try To Remember

Words by Tom Jones
Music by Harvey Schmidt

Registration 10

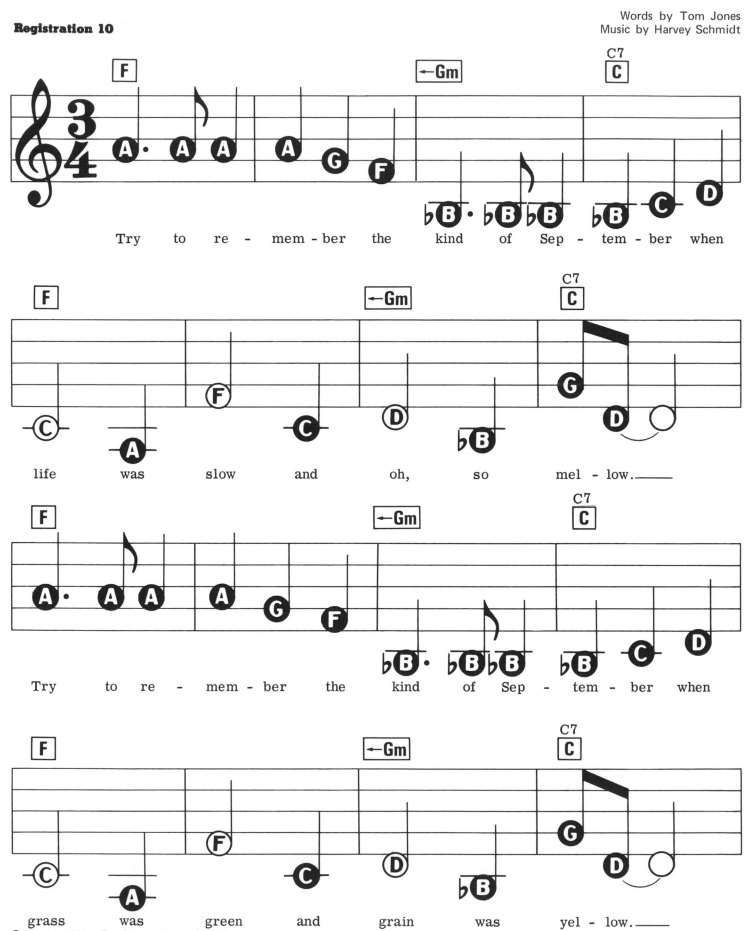

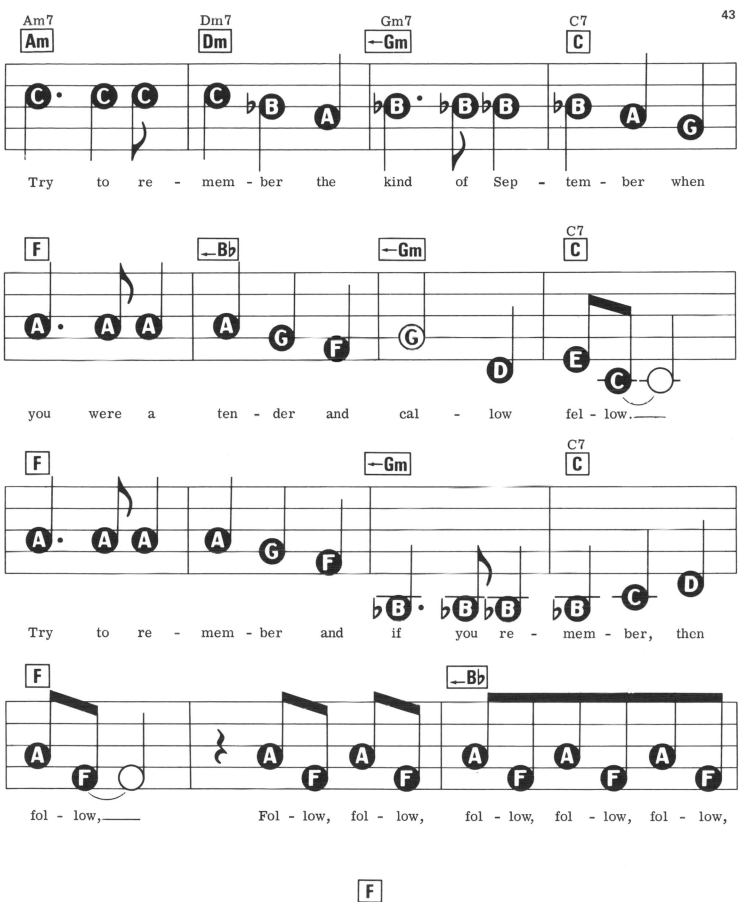

43

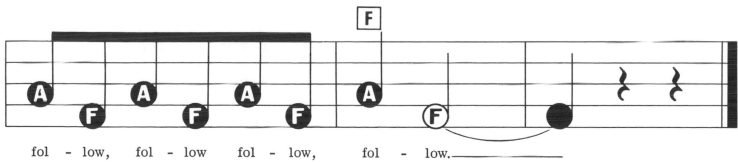

Yellow Days

Registration 1

English Words by Alan Bernstein
Spanish Words and Music by Alvaro Carrillo

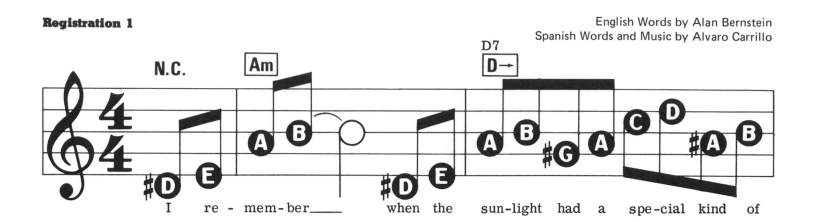

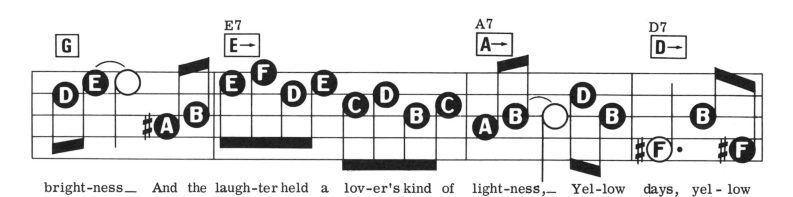

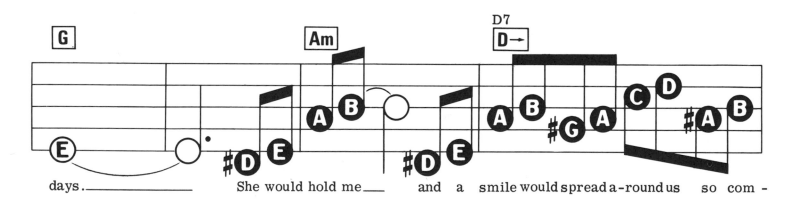

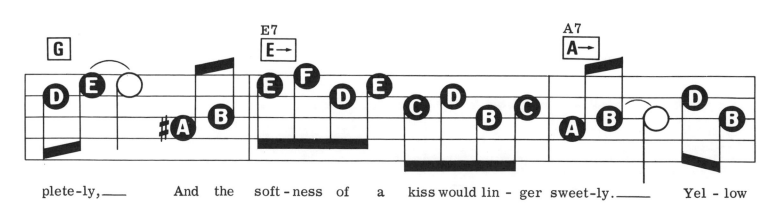

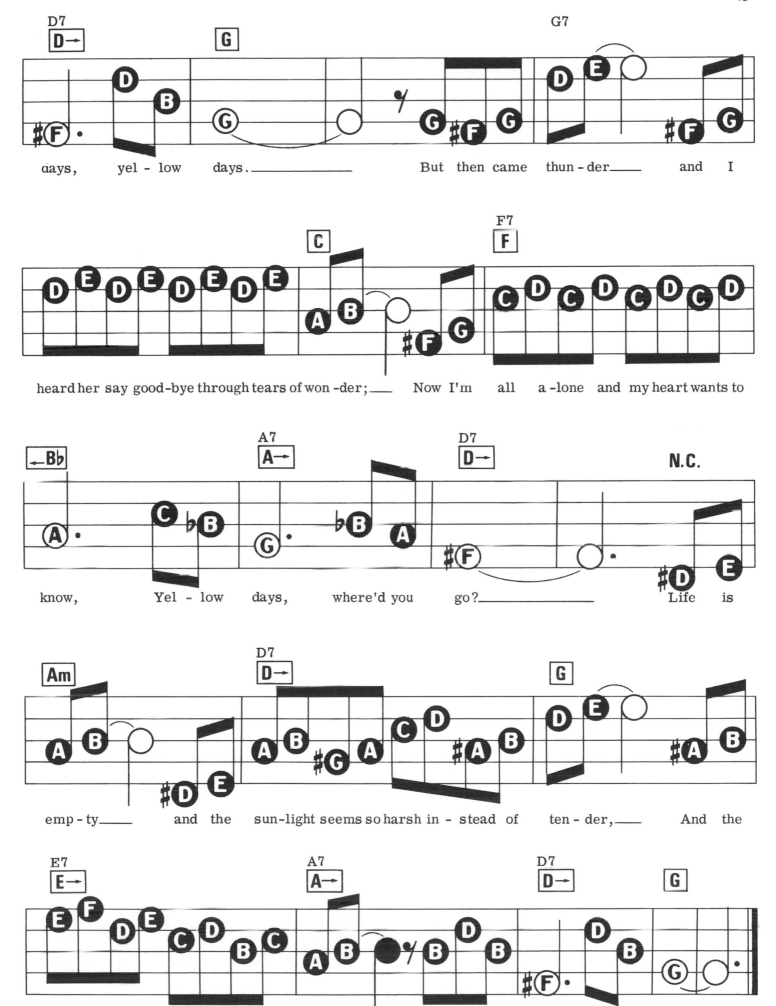

Guitar Chord Chart

To use the E-Z Play TODAY Guitar Chord chart, simply find the **letter name** of the chord at the top of the chart, and the **kind of chord** (Major, Minor, etc.) in the column at the left. Read down and across to find the correct chord. Suggested fingering has been indicated, but feel free to use alternate fingering.

	C	D♭	D	E♭	E	F
MAJOR						
MINOR (m)						
7TH (7)						
MINOR 7TH (m7)						

	F♯	G	A♭	A	B♭	B
MAJOR						
MINOR (m)						
7TH (7)						
MINOR 7TH (m7)						

Chord Speller Chart
of Standard Chord Positions

For those who play standard chord positions, all chords used in the E-Z Play TODAY music arrangements are shown here in their most commonly used chord positions. Suggested fingering is also indicated, but feel free to use alternate fingering.

CHORD FAMILY Abbrev.	MAJOR	MINOR (m)	7TH (7)	MINOR 7TH (m7)
C	5 2 1 G-C-E	5 2 1 G-C-E♭	5 3 2 1 G-B♭-C-E	5 3 2 1 G-B♭-C-E♭
D♭	5 2 1 A♭-D♭-F	5 2 1 A♭-D♭-E	5 3 2 1 A♭-B-D♭-F	5 3 2 1 A♭-B-D♭-E
D	5 3 1 F♯-A-D	5 2 1 A-D-F	5 3 2 1 F♯-A-C-D	5 3 2 1 A-C-D-F
E♭	5 3 1 G-B♭-E♭	5 3 1 G♭-B♭-E♭	5 3 2 1 G-B♭-D♭-E♭	5 3 2 1 G♭-B♭-D♭-E♭
E	5 3 1 G♯-B-E	5 3 1 G-B-E	5 3 2 1 G♯-B-D-E	5 3 2 1 G-B-D-E
F	4 2 1 A-C-F	4 2 1 A♭-C-F	5 3 2 1 A-C-E♭-F	5 3 2 1 A♭-C-E♭-F
F♯	4 2 1 F♯-A♯-C♯	4 2 1 F♯-A-C♯	5 3 2 1 F♯-A♯-C♯-E	5 3 2 1 F♯-A-C♯-E
G	5 3 1 G-B-D	5 3 1 G-B♭-D	5 3 2 1 G-B-D-F	5 3 2 1 G-B♭-D-F
A♭	4 2 1 A♭-C-E♭	4 2 1 A♭-B-E♭	5 3 2 1 A♭-C-E♭-G♭	5 3 2 1 A♭-B-E♭-G♭
A	4 2 1 A-C♯-E	4 2 1 A-C-E	5 4 2 1 G-A-C♯-E	5 4 2 1 G-A-C-E
B♭	4 2 1 B♭-D-F	4 2 1 B♭-D♭-F	5 4 2 1 A♭-B♭-D-F	5 4 2 1 A♭-B♭-D♭-F
B	5 2 1 F♯-B-D♯	5 2 1 F♯-B-D	5 3 2 1 F♯-A-B-D♯	5 3 2 1 F♯-A-B-D